Have and Have Not

A Kid's Guide to Understanding Money

Introduction

- *Do you have kids and are wondering how to introduce them to the concept of money?*

- *Are you struggling to help your children understand the value of money?*

If you've answered yes to the question above, please read on because this book is here to help you teach your children the value of money in ways they can understand and value.

Parents often think that children are too young to learn about the value of money. Thus, many parents often never teach their children how to make great financial decisions, only for the child to finally reach adulthood and realize that they lack basic financial literacy.

Then, a few years into their jobs, the parents keep wondering why their child is not making any progress in life or why their child lives paycheck to paycheck and struggles to live a decent life despite perhaps having a decently paying job. The child struggles to pay for their needs and wants, mortgage, perhaps buying a good car, going for the desired vacation, or dining at that fancy restaurant. Why? Because there is no money to pay for it.

And so, as a parent, you watch as your child wakes up each morning, going to a job that you thought would earn them wealth, and watch as they grow older without achieving many of the dreams they wanted to achieve because money seems not to want to stay in their pockets for long.

So, was the idea that you can build wealth through working hard false? Is it really and truly impossible to build wealth by just working without making crazy investments?

It is very easy to think that perhaps your child simply got into the wrong career that doesn't pay them enough. But looking around, we see that many people are working well-paying jobs that would be a dream for many others, yet they still live paycheck to paycheck.

Thus, we can safely assume that the issue is not about how much money they make but what they do with the paycheck once it lands in their hands. Unfortunately, their childhood did not teach them the many financial and money management lessons they now need as adults.

It's very important to mention that I'm not writing this book because I know everything there is to know about finances, and I am very wealthy. Rather, I am writing this book because the lessons I learned about money as an adult came a little late, and if I had learned them earlier in life, I would have made even better financial decisions sooner.

This book is a detailed guide on lessons parents can teach their children about money early in life and give them a head start in the march towards wealth accumulation, like how the wealthy do it. The idealogy behind this book is to equip you with financial literacy skills and knowledge you can pass on to your kids to ensure they are financially responsible, regardless of their income levels.

So, if you read this book and diligently apply its lessons to your children's lives, you could help them become people who continue the journey towards building generational wealth and individuals who eliminate the wrong mindset around money, income, and how to manage them. No longer would they be held back by thoughts that they aren't earning enough.

If this has piqued your interest, read on and learn how to give your kids a financial literacy head start.

Table of Content

Introduction _____ 2

Chapter 1: Rich Kid, Poor Kid: How Different Are They, Really? _____ 9

    Where The Differences Come In _____ 10

Chapter 2: Changing the Mindset: For the Love of Money _____ 13

    The Moral Conundrum: Is Money Dirty and Evil? _____ 14

    Of Marbles, Money, and Empty Jars _____ 16

    Valuing What We Have _____ 18

    Ways of Shifting the Mindset _____ 20

Chapter 3: Parental Influence on Money Habits _____ 26

    Teaching Credit, Loans, and the Importance of Payback Practices _____ 28

    Being in The Black and The Red _____ 35

How to Teach Kids to Build Good Habits to Keep Them in the Black _____ 37

Chapter 4: Budgeting and Wise Spending 42

Budgeting as a Net Positive for Finances _____ 43

The Value of Saving: Simple Sayings, Simple Savings_____ 49

The Power of a Dollar a Day _____ 51

Chapter 5: Understanding Expenses_____ 55

What are Expenses? _____ 55

Categorizing Expenses _____ 56

Importance of Delayed Gratification _____ 60

Chapter 6: Unconventional Wisdom on Chores: Lessons on Building Wealth from Chores_____ 63

Chores Are More Than Just Chores _____ 64

Building the Spirit of Commitment Through Chores _____ 70

Chapter 7: Dreaming Big: Being Unlimited in Thoughts and Action _____ 76

Why Having Big Dreams Matters in Building Wealth_____ 78

How To Help Kids Dream Big _____ 82

Chapter 8: Homeschool Money and Life Skills _____ 89

The Advantage of Homeschooling in Finances 90

Financial Lessons to Teach Your Child in Homeschooling _____ 93

Chapter 9: Building a Long-Term Perspective on Financial Decisions _____ 103

Investing: Putting Long-Term Financial Thinking in Action _____ 106

Lessons from Successful Investors _____ 111

Chapter 10: Trust Funds and The Introduction of Roth IRA _____ 118

Deciphering Trust Funds _____ 119

Understanding and Breaking Down Roth IRA 122

Benefits of Roth IRA _____127

Chapter 11: The Daddy Excuse–Family Background Shouldn't Stop Wealth Building _____ 131

How to Help Children Break Free From The Daddy Excuse _____133

Conclusion_____143

Other Books By The Author _____145

Chapter 1: Rich Kid, Poor Kid: How Different Are They, Really?

"The schools of the rich prepare their children for the world; the schools of the poor prepare them for the factories."

Paulo Freire

Growing up, I often thought that wealthy children and the rest of us children were so different that we may as well have existed in different galaxies.

I had often assumed that any child from a wealthy background and I would never get along, no matter what. But all that would change this one time when I got to spend considerable time with a boy from a well-off family.

This boy had a quite expensive-looking action figure, which he carried with him everywhere he went. As I later learned during our time together that afternoon, it was his most prized possession, and he always had his action figure with him.

I never got to play with the action figure, but the boy let me feel it. However, every time I would have it for a while, he would ask for it and put it back into a little bag, close the zipper, and stuff that bag safely into his pocket.

I was disappointed that we couldn't play with the toy, but despite all that, we still found a lot to talk about —to my absolute shock.

We bonded over mutual interests, dreams, and desires for the future, and of course, over how much school sucked and how we could not wait to be out. I was shocked because never in my life had I imagined that I would have that much in common with someone from a well-off family.

That day, I went home with my mind occupied by deep thoughts about how much children, no matter their background, were all the same or more similar than I had thought.

Where The Differences Come In

While at a fundamental level, a rich kid and a poor kid all have a lot in common, the unfortunate reality is that when it comes to how both engage with money and valuable possessions, the differences start to set in.

My meet-up with the boy from the rich family taught me a lot about the importance of valuing and enjoying what you have without unnecessarily risking losing it.

The way he cared for his action figure toy and how careful he was even when he let people touch it taught me a valuable lesson on how to value what I had, and that is where the difference between rich children and poor children comes in.

This story clearly shows the differences between how affluent and less affluent children relate to money. Because of growing up in situations where they lack a lot, less affluent children often never learn how to truly care for what they have.

It won't be that they will be careless, but rather, due to a lack of exposure to the importance of caring for what is valuable, they will struggle to know how to care for the valuables in their life.

Meanwhile, because of growing up in abundance, most children from affluent families learn early on how to be responsible with what they own and how to care for what they have, even as they also seek out more and more.

These different degrees of exposure collectively determine how each child grows up to view money and possessions.

When they eventually own something, those who grow up without any teachings on valuing what you own—because there wasn't much to own anyway—will often overcompensate, which will come in the form of overspending if it's money or over-attachment to possessions.

Meanwhile, someone brought up in abundance is well-versed in wise spending and proper secure attachment to their possessions. And it is on the attitudes around money and possessions that parents or less privileged children should look to change how their children think.

Chapter 2: Changing the Mindset: For the Love of Money

"Money will only make you more of what you already are."

T Harv Eker

I know that many of us grew up with the belief that money is all kinds of evil and that loving it is one of the worst things that you could ever do. Many of us learned early on that we could never openly show or say we loved money.

This idea then became so ingrained in our heads that many of us are actually scared of earning more or making more and admitting we desire a higher-paying job than our current one because we fear social judgment for desiring more money.

This kind of negative attitude towards money is one of the biggest reasons why many of us never build wealth, and if we pass on this idea to children, they will also have a hard time accumulating wealth in their adult years.

But is money that evil?

The Moral Conundrum: Is Money Dirty and Evil?

The verse on 1 Timothy 6:10 is where the saying *For the love of money is the root of all evil* comes from, and many of us have taken this saying to mean we should not pursue wealth or love money.

Thus, this view of money being an evil entity in and of itself has led to many of us growing up with ingrained ideas that we should never desire to have more money or buy more things because of the belief that money is evil.

However, when we read the next verses of the chapter, we can see that the verse is actually against greediness rather than simply being against us loving money.

There is a way you can love money and desire to build wealth that does not show greed, and this is how you ought to teach your children to love money.

So, this brings us back to the question: Is money itself evil?

Well, let us look at this situation.

Two people are extremely wealthy. Both live in the same community and while they also live around other wealthy people, there are considerable problems in other, less wealthy parts of the community.

One of these wealthy people uses a significant part of their wealth to make life-changing improvements. They dig wells for the community, build schools and hospitals, and improve people's homes.

Meanwhile, the other wealthy person does none of this. Instead, they spend their money throwing parties, buying luxury cars & private jets, and buying property around the community, even if it comes at the expense of others.

On the one hand, one wealthy person uses their money to do a lot of good in the community, while the other person uses the money for their own selfish needs.

This story is a lesson that money, in and of itself, is neither dirty nor clean; it is neither evil nor good. Rather, what matters is what we choose to do with money.

Money is nothing but a piece of paper onto which our economies attach value. Money is neutral. As many would say, 'Money just is.'

Thus, let your children know that the notion that money is evil or dirty is false and wrong. Let them know that money's value lies in how we choose to use it.

The notion that money is dirty and evil often shapes the fact that many of us do not desire to build wealth or at least have enough to live comfortable lives.

Meanwhile, children from rich families usually learn the value of money and why they should guard it like their life depends on it—because it does. Their folks teach them how to care for the money they have, how to save, how to make more of it, and how to spend it.

So, teach your child the value of money as though they were from a rich family. Let them understand that money can be a force for good, and this will help them have a positive relationship with their finances in the future when you are not around to lecture them.

But how, then, do you go about shifting the mindset around money?

Of Marbles, Money, and Empty Jars

In chapter one, I narrated a story about a boy who owned an action figure he considered his most prized possession.

That reminded me of another story I read about a boy who had marbles he would put in a bag and take with him everywhere. This boy was so proud of and loved his marbles so much that he neither took them out to play with nor let anyone play with them.

Instead, whenever he would take them out, it would be to count and admire them. The boy never played with them, not even once. Close by was another boy who neither had marbles nor a bag. This boy wished to one day own his bag of marbles.

So, figuring out his disadvantage, this second boy began working hard, and soon enough, he earned enough money to purchase a nice bag where he would put his marbles.

This boy took care of the bag, dreaming that one day he would also find his marbles, which he would then use to play with his friends.

However, on the other hand, the boy with the marbles did not care for the marble bag itself, and soon enough, the bag developed a hole in the bottom seam. One by one, his marbles kept falling.

Meanwhile, the second boy began to find these beautiful marbles, and one by one, he added them into his bag until it was full. Then, he took his marbles out and used them to play with his friends.

Because the first boy did not care for his marble bag nor play with his marbles, he ended up losing them, while the second boy took care of his bag and played with his marbles, thus enjoying their value.

Valuing What We Have

The parable above is a great story of two people with two widely contrasting attitudes about what they own and how this then impacts their lives.

In the first story, the first boy has something he finds valuable: his marbles. That was good. However, what made him foolish was that he never extracted the full value of the marbles he had and never took care of the bag in which he kept the marbles. That then resulted in him losing his marbles.

This story is a metaphor for what it is like to grow up and never learn how to take care of your finances. When you do not know how to care for and extract maximum value from what you have, you risk losing it.

When it comes to teaching your child about money, that means when you raise a child and never teach them the value of money or how to spend it wisely, they risk losing it before they even extract the value in it.

Meanwhile, another lesson we learned from the second child is valuing the little we have and being confident that we will have more added to us.

The second boy bought a bag for his anticipated marbles despite not knowing if he would get them. He simply acted on faith and confidence in his capacity and ability to find a solution.

Thus, when teaching children about finances, help them understand the value of whatever little they have, even if it seems pointless. Finding great value in even the smallest things helps us build the mindset required to accumulate wealth and become rich.

Teach your children to value an aged penny just as much as they would value a gold coin. If, for example, a child gets a penny every once in a while and they have an empty jar, if they keep putting a penny into the jar each time they get it, then over time, that jar will fill with pennies, which will be of a lot of value to the child.

However, if each time the child gets a penny, they do not put it in the jar, and then even if the pennies are golden, over time, they will not have a lot of value to the child because the jar will still be empty.

The value of something is not in its composition but rather in how well we manage it. No matter how old it is, a penny symbolizes how small things can add up over time to something large. When a child learns how to value an old coin, they will always and forever be grateful and care for it like it's the most prized possession in the world.

When you teach the child how to find value in aged coins, the lessons will be useful when they get their hands on gold coins. Because no matter what people may try to tell you, if one does not value the little they have, they will not value the much they gain.

Ways of Shifting the Mindset

"You can change your health, you can change your relationships, you can change your income, you can change anything."

Bob Proctor

Below are some practical ways to teach a child how to change their views on money and wealth:

- **De-romanticize the 'just enough' mentality:** I've noticed that most parents from 'poor families' have this 'just enough' mentality that romanticizes the idea of having 'just enough for everything we need.' If you want your kids to develop a healthy money and wealth mindset, you should detach yourself from this narrow wealth belief and do your best to de-romanticize it in your household.

Since kids learn from examples, you should become uncomfortable with the idea of being happy with 'just enough' because such a mindset only gets you the absolute minimum. Instead, motivate them—and yourself—to adopt an abundant money mindset by championing the idea that the universe is abundant enough that we can all have more than enough to live our best lives. This way, when your kids see you striving to have more than enough, they will know that they should also always strive to have more than enough for everything they could ever need—and then some.

- **We all can build wealth:** Teach your child early in life that the fact that they are not from a wealthy family does not doom them to being unable to accumulate wealth or money. There is a thinking among parents that because they aren't wealthy enough, they do not have anything to teach their children about money.

That is inherently false. No matter your income level, you can teach your child how to make correct financial decisions that can help them improve their financial situation.

- **Money begets money**: A friend of mine once said to me that he always strove never to lack even a cent in his bank account because if he were ever to get to zero, that would be the end of him. His thinking was that, even with a little money in the bank, there was always a possibility that he could use it to make more money, even when he had no idea how to do it. Thus, let the child also know that they should always strive to keep some money away and not spend all the money they have, no matter how small they think it is.

- **Build a saving culture**: Many people think saving starts in adulthood, but learning how to save starts in childhood. Thus, start teaching your child how to save the moment they are old enough to need and want to carry some pocket money. Sit them down and ask them to create a plan on how they want to spend the money and what percentage of it they want to save. Then, go through the plan together as you make changes and teach them how to make a better budget next time.

- **Money is a tool for empowerment:** Let the child understand that money is a tool that will help them feel empowered. Money helps us feel free; it also builds our confidence because with it in our pockets and bank accounts, we can do things we want to do, live the life we wish to live, and buy the things we want.

- **Their dreams and aspirations directly tie back to money:** Let the child know that achieving their dreams and aspirations will always tie back to having money to actualize those wishes. It doesn't matter whether that dream is making art or altruism. Let them know they will need money to live a comfortable life and achieve their dreams. Knowing they will need money for other pursuits outside of making money will help improve their financial choices.

- **Loving money is not a bad thing**: Teach your children that they should not be afraid of admitting that they would love to have more money and pursue it. Of course, you should teach them not to be greedy and not to put money above everything else in life; teach them to value other things such as relationships with loved ones and knowledge and wisdom more, but also let them know that no one should make them feel bad for wanting to build wealth or make more money.

With this understanding, we can create conditions that allow our kids to take lessons on financial responsibility much more seriously.

Now, as a parent who may have grown up with the notion that money is evil and dirty, these lessons might seem as though they are very superficial, and it may seem like you are teaching your child to be vain and shallow, but you should remember rich kids are getting these lessons.

Somewhere in the mansions of gated communities, parents are teaching their children how to love and care for the money they have. Parents are giving their children money and letting them learn how to spend and budget it.

These rich children will then go out into the world, and because they have a head start over your child, they will know how to make better financial decisions that will lead them to more wealth accumulation. Remember the point of money-getting money? Rich children building on their parent's wealth aptly illustrates that principle.

These kids can capably make these choices because their parents were not worried about being seen as vain or shallow; they just wanted to secure their children's financial future.

And speaking of teaching children to love and value money, your habits should also be a lesson for them.

Chapter 3: Parental Influence on Money Habits

"Don't worry that children never listen to you; worry that they are always watching you."

Robert Fulghum

Did you know that, in some countries, when two people marry and one partner dies with debt, the debt transfers to the remaining spouse, who then has to bear the arduous task of offsetting their partner's debt?

On the other hand, if the remaining spouse dies without clearing the debt, the debt trickles down to their children if they have any. The logic behind this idea is that since assets are inherited, why should debts not be inherited?

That was one of the most jarring things I have ever learned, and it spoke deeply to how many of us do not see the impact our debts have on our children.

I have met many people who often take pride in having a lot of debt out of thinking that rich people will often have debt, and thus, if rich people have debt, then why not them?

However, the reality is that, due to the numerous assets and financial muscle they have, debt is often a good thing for rich people because it will often signify the fact that they have great credit scores and, thus, can afford to take debts, knowing they have enough assets to offset them.

And when it comes to their children, rich people know they can agree to an irrevocable trust fund. In this agreement, the rich person and the creditor agree that certain assets will be secure from debt collection in the future, unless under certain circumstances.

With this arrangement, a rich person can put their child's inheritance in it and prevent these assets from repossession to offset any existing debt. As we can see, when it comes to their kids, rich people often find ways to go around debt, a luxury that the rest of us do not have.

Thus, as a parent, this realization should jolt you awake and make you decide to improve how you sort out your finances and teach your child how to take care of their assets and deal with debt.

And how do you do that?

Teaching Credit, Loans, and the Importance of Payback Practices

Loans and credits are two very important parts of our existence. I do not believe we have a single adult who has gone through life without taking a loan or buying something on credit.

It doesn't matter whether the loan is from a friend, a shylock, or from a bank or loan institution. We have all needed a loan to do something; thus, loans and credits are all part of our existence.

Consequently, it is very important to teach your child about this because of the value of loans and credit in our lives and finances.

So, how do you teach kids the importance of credit, loans, and payback practices?

Introduction To Credit

Credit is a means of living that is very common in many parts of the world, and thus, any parent who wants their child to make great financial decisions should teach them about it.

For example, you can use house chores to teach them about credit. A child in middle school or their early teen is certainly someone you can sit down and explain this concept to.

So, for example, let us say you both have an arrangement that if they complete house chores, you give them a little allowance. So, for example, sometimes, if you do not have money, you can agree with them to complete the chores, and then you will pay them later.

Let them understand that this is sometimes how money is. They will not always have money to purchase things they need or want, which is where credit comes in.

Alternatively, you can also go together to the supermarket or any place where you use your credit card and teach them how credit works in real time. When you purchase credit, let them know you are buying things on credit without paying for them at that moment but that your account credit will reflect the money you should be paying for whatever you are purchasing.

"So, what if you don't pay back? What will happen?" They will ask.

Here is where you also now teach them the consequences of not committing to paying the credit. Here is where you teach them about a credit score.

What is a credit score? Explain to them what those numbers from 300 to 850 mean. Why does a high score mean a good credit score? Let them know that when they repay their credit and do it on time, they improve their credit score. A good credit score means they can access higher credit facilities at better rates; thus, they can use the credit money to improve their financial situation.

However, it is also important to let the child know that while having access to higher credit is good, they should not use it to live beyond their means.

For example, using good credit to fund frivolous spending habits will only sink them further into poverty instead of providing them with a path to building wealth.

A good credit score is a means for them to make the purchases they need when they do not have enough to pay for them, but they will still have to pay for it later. Thus, spending within your credit and income limits is part of good financial habits that they should learn.

Understanding Loans

Loans are one of the most important financial concepts we have in the world today, and they help many of us live properly and make those purchases we might not have made otherwise.

Your child will wonder how a loan differs from credit. Let the child know that a loan is a type of credit where you get a lump sum of money to make a specific purchase, such as a house or loan.

Unlike credit, a loan doesn't involve making a purchase you commit to paying later. With a loan, you take the money and use it, then pay the money back later.

The following is an example to explain the concept better.

Let us say your child wants to buy something for themselves; for this example, let's use a pair of sunglasses. If their pocket money is insufficient to buy the glasses, they can come to you to give them some amount to make the purchase, and then they have loaned money from you.

However, let them know that loaning money will often have a payback agreement. For example, since you know they do not have a source of income, the means of payback can be that they do house chores for a given amount of time without pay, equivalent to the allowance you give them so that it covers the loan.

For bigger purchases, let them know they should take loans to do bigger and better things and avoid taking loans to purchase things they can live without (wants). They could take loans to start a business or buy a home or a car that helps them get to work.

Advise them against taking loans to go on holiday or buy a very expensive gadget like a smartphone. In short, if the purchase does not directly link back to their source of income, they should consider not taking it because that would make payback difficult and could sink them further into the debt trap.

Importance of Payback

Many people often think they are on the winning side by not paying back their owed debts. I have met people, some of them my age, who seem to take pride in not repaying their debt, often trying to be clever in avoiding the debt collectors, and that is not the type of character you would want your child to have.

Explain to the child why paying back their loan is important through relatable analogies. For example, let us say they borrow a book they do not have from someone else. Borrowing that book is equivalent to borrowing a loan.

After reading the book and using it as they desire, they should hand it back soon after completing it. A consequence of giving the book back in good condition after borrowing is maintaining a good relationship with the friend, and this good relationship means that if they borrow from the friend next time, they will still get the book. The same is true for loan repayment.

Let the child know that when they repay a loan they took within the agreed repayment period, they get a good credit score that gives them access to not just the loan but to higher loans in the future.

Teach them the importance of a payback plan that will not dent their pocket as they service a loan or pay a credit. Having a plan teaches them responsibility when they get the loan and lets them know if they are trying to borrow beyond their ability to repay.

For example, teach them that if they take a loan in the future, they should be able to make monthly payments to the loan while also still living comfortably. If they make a repayment plan that requires them to make very big sacrifices in their lifestyle to furnish it, they should consider not taking that loan.

Introduce Interest

The concept of interest is a very important part of loans and credits. Thus, explain to them that borrowing a loan or credit often comes with an additional cost called interest.

Let them know that the longer they go without paying back the loan or credit, the more the interest increases, meaning they risk paying much more in the end.

Here is an example of how to teach them about interests.

Let us say they borrowed money from you to make a given purchase, and the payback was that they would do chores for, let's say, a few days without allowance as payback. You can then ask them to do an extra chore, which could be the interest.

And if they fail to complete the chores as agreed, you can add extra chores to them until they complete it all.

This lesson is important because children should understand that when they grow up, they will have to do more than pay back their loans; their creditors will also charge them extra as a service fee. The more they fail to repay the loan, the higher the interest on the loan grows. And just like house chores, the more they let the interest grow, the harder it will be to complete the repayment.

Being in The Black and The Red

I mentioned how your child needs to understand that while credit and loans are vital tools that can significantly help them through their financial journey, they should not be beyond their ability to pay.

And this is where we introduce the concept of being in the red and being in the black.

Perhaps even you as a parent might not understand this concept because these words are only common in financial settings. But these phrases represent two very simple financial concepts.

Let us say your source of income is enough to get you by comfortably. You do not suffer from financial issues most of the time, and you have enough in your bank for some luxuries here and there and very little in terms of debts. When you live life like this, we can say you are in the black.

Conversely, when someone is constantly in debt and their income is much lower than their expenditure, and when someone seems to be getting by through more loans and credits than income, we consider that person to be in the red.

Understanding these financial concepts is critical in financial literacy, and your child needs to understand this if they are going to make good financial decisions.

There are a few ways you can teach the child this concept.

Now, let us say that the child has a piggy bank. Let us say the piggy bank is full, and you decide to break it because the child wants to buy something.

When they count the money and find that it is more than the money they plan to spend, it means they have a surplus and will have some money left from the purchase. That is what being in the black means. It means having enough money to cover your needs while still having a surplus of it to do other things with.

Let your children know that this should be how they should live: they should strive to earn more than they can spend to ensure they have enough surplus money for other things beyond their basic needs.

On the other end, if breaking the piggy bank reveals they do not have enough for their intended purchase, they are in the red. That means they need to figure out how to earn more money to fill in the amount to make their desired purchase.

When in the red, they barely have enough to get by, which leads to constantly borrowing and repaying. That eliminates any possibility of building wealth because when money comes in, it'll immediately go to repaying their loans. That means they will borrow more for their needs, leaving them in a perpetual debt cycle.

You can also teach them this concept when going to the store. Let us say they have some of their money with them. Ask them to select items they desire. Then, make the calculations of the price of those items. Then, calculate the amount of money they have on them.

If the money is enough to make the purchase and leave some extra, they are in the black, which is good. However, if their preferred items cost more than the money they have, then they are in the red because they will need to figure out how to cover the extra expenses, and that will mean borrowing money, whether it be from you or someone else.

How to Teach Kids to Build Good Habits to Keep Them in the Black

Once a child is well aware of and understands the concept of being in the black and being in the red, it is time to teach them positive behavior that will help them build better financial habits that will keep them in the black.

We call this teaching paradigm positive reinforcement, and it is a great way to help cement money lessons in a child's mind.

Here is how to go about it:

- **Be an example:** According to Rachel Cruze, a bestselling finance author and expert, children start forming core money habits and beliefs between the ages of 6 and 12. Because of this, it's fundamentally important to remember that your kids are always watching your habits, learning from them, and using them to create their core beliefs. That's why you should be a great example. After all, if you have lousy money habits, the little 'always watching eyes' will subconsciously absorb them.

    For example, if you never create a shopping list, make impulse purchases all the time, or if you and your partner are always arguing about money, your kids will learn that such things are normal. That's why you should be deliberate with your spending habits; that way, your kids will absorb good core habits from your interaction with money.

- **Commissions over allowances:** Instead of giving your kids an allowance—you know, because you can afford it and want to give them one because you never had it—focus on commissions. For example, instead of giving allowances for chores, give commissions based on how well they do their chores; you can even use a grading system. Patrick Bet-David, for example, gives his kids commissions for doing growth-oriented things, like reading a specific number of pages of a self-help book.

- **Create a reward system**: Children respond very well to the reward system, so this is your best bet to teach them about credit and being in the red or black. For example, you can reward them with extra allowance if they stay in the black after each purchase, meaning they have money left after spending or making a purchase.

When they go into the red, they don't get any extra allowance they can save. When you reward them for making the correct financial decisions, such as purchasing something within their means, you incentivize them to stick to that behavior.

- **Embrace a culture of saving:** We have already touched on the importance of helping kids change their money and wealth mindset by making a saving culture part of your family ethos. This is one of the most important things you can do to help your kids develop good money habits because when your kids see you putting money aside for saving, perhaps even as the first thing on your budget—you have to pay yourself first, right?—they'll start taking note of the importance of doing so.

  For example, if you give your kids percentage-based commissions for doing their homework or studying for a specific amount of time, motivate them to save a percentage of it, perhaps in a saving jar, before they account for other expenses or consider using it. You can use a three-jar system—one jar for saving, another for spending, and one for giving—to motivate kids to embrace your family's saving ethos.

- **Role-playing:** Engage in a role-playing game where you ask them to manage a budget for a made-up scenario. For example, you could play a game where you give them a certain amount of money to spend. Ask them to draft a budget, covering all the necessities and some extra expenditure here and there while still managing to have some amount left. You could go further and have a set amount you want them to have remaining.

These role-playing games further reinforce the concepts you are trying to teach them. Using real-life examples makes it easier for children to understand what loans, credits, interests, and payments are. You also make the concepts of being in the black and being in the red a lot more relatable and engaging, making it easier for the lessons to stick.

Chapter 4: Budgeting and Wise Spending

"Don't tell me where your priorities are. Show me where you spend your money, and I'll tell you what they are."

James W. Frick

One of the most important things anyone can ever do with their money is to establish a budget they can stick to and spend money wisely.

I remember when I was younger. I often thought that a budget was this big bad thing that people did that limited their freedom to use and spend their money.

Because I wasn't very well aware of what a budget was, I had learned to view it negatively as something that limited spending. After all, I only ever heard of the word budget when money was tight, and this often meant cutting back from doing things we enjoy and, instead, strictly using the money for covering needs.

I know this view on budgeting is not unique to me. Many of us have grown up in families where we didn't have much. Thus, having a budget felt like this big bad thing that stopped us from fully enjoying money.

That could perhaps explain why some adults do not value budgeting much and instead 'wing it' when spending their money.

However, now that you are reading this book, I am certain your view on budgeting has changed. You view it as a net positive in your finances and want to teach your child budgeting lessons but do not know how.

Well, let us look at ways you can introduce budgeting to your children as a good thing for their pockets.

Budgeting as a Net Positive for Finances

People are not born hating budgeting; instead, they hate it because its usage when they were children was usually during times of lack. Thus, as adults, they associate budgeting with a lack.

Thus, as a parent, this is the time to introduce budgeting to the child as a positive thing, and there are various ways to do this. These include the following:

Make Kids Part of the Budgeting Process

That might seem like taking things too far too early, but the best way to introduce a child to budgeting is by introducing them to the family budget.

When making the family budget, invite your child over. A middle school or pre-teen child is old enough to understand basic concepts of what you will teach them, so you aren't teaching them something complex beyond their years. After inviting them over, quiz them by asking questions like:

What is a budget, and what does it do? When do we use a budget? What do they think about budgeting: is it a good or bad thing? Why is budgeting important? And similar questions.

Then, inform them that you are also making a budget for the family and want them to observe and learn. Have an amount that can be a reference point. I know many parents will freak out and think, *'What if the child sees it and thinks we have a lot of money?'*

When you teach your lessons right, whether they think you have a lot of money or not will become irrelevant as they implement your financial ideas.

Once you have the child with you, making the family budget, make them see the effort you put into sub-dividing money for everything. Let them know the importance of estimating how much you want to spend because it helps curb overspending.

Many rich parents will often make their children understand the value of money even if they have a lot of it. So, you can do that, too, considering it is in short supply on your end.

Besides, when your child learns about the family budget, they become aware of the money available and not available for certain purchases, which makes it unlikely that they will ask for more than you can provide.

Teach Kids to Draft Shopping Lists

Aside from understanding the family budget, let them also know that it is important to have a list of what they intend to buy when going to the supermarket.

When drafting your shopping list, let the child help you with it. Ask them to check for the necessities around the house that are in short supply or out of stock as you write them down. Or they could also be writing them down as you identify the items.

Make them understand that having a shopping list helps them remember what they need to buy, thus reducing trips to and fro the supermarket or convenience store and also helps stop them from overspending through impulse buying.

As you walk in the supermarket, let them understand that the stores use a design structure that makes it easier to walk around and spend more. Thus, a shopping list is a way of ensuring they stay true to the script.

After placing every necessary item in the basket or trolley, if they are still in the black according to the shopping budget, they can consider buying something else, perhaps a toy or a snack.

Budgeting with Their Money

As you teach them financial responsibility on a larger scale, ensure they also understand that budgeting isn't just something they should do for big money and big responsibilities.

Let them know they can also create a budget for the small amounts of money they have for themselves. For example, let us say they have filled their piggy bank and want to spend the money. Once they have cracked the piggy bank, help them count the money.

After calculating the total amount, ask them to pull out their notebook and pen and write down a budget detailing what they intend to do with the money. If a desired purchase exceeds the amount, tell them it is okay to move the purchase to another time. Or they can make that purchase the target for their next savings.

The child should know that no amount of money is too small to budget for. This understanding will teach them to value that rusty old coin just as much as they value the gold coin. They will learn to value a coin as much as they value the dollar.

Make the budget-creating process fun and lively to ensure the lessons stick and the child doesn't get distracted. For example, they can use color coding for different purchases.

Purchases they consider urgent and within the amount they have can be in green and be at the top of the budgeting page. That could be school items such as pencils, pens, drawing books, etc.

Purchases that aren't urgent but are still within their purchasing power can be in yellow and be below the purchases colored yellow. These could include a toy or gadget they like, clothing or jewelry, etc.

Then, purchases above the amount they have can be in red. Anything in the red gives you a rare opportunity to reinforce the lesson on loans, credits, and payback. Perhaps you can both agree you will make the purchase for them and in return, they will do an extra chore.

The different colors let the child know how to prioritize the money they have and can help them understand that spending money on a budget can still be fun and free.

Spending Should Bring Value

Another lesson on budgeting is that your child needs to understand that when they spend money, they must ensure they get value in return.

Tell the child, *"Money is useful not only when you spend it, but spend it on things that bring value to you."*

Let the child know that, for example, candy might be sweet and seem like a good way to spend money, but spending too much on candy represents wasted money.

Teach them that candy has no value to the body and, thus, should not be seen as a very important purchase. They should only buy candy with pocket change, not their main money.

For the main money, their priority should be on spending it on things that will give value for much longer than just a few minutes of sugary pleasure. Money spent on a toy can be more valuable than any money spent on candy because at least they can play with it for weeks, months, or even years.

This way, the child learns not just how to spend money but also how to extract maximum value from it.

The Value of Saving: Simple Sayings, Simple Savings

While discussing budgeting, let the child also understand that keeping aside money is also important. When creating a budget, let them understand that they should also aim to have some cash set aside as savings. Teaching kids about saving is an excellent way to reinforce the value of money.

Savings have many benefits for everyone; below are the benefits of savings you should ensure your child knows:

- **Introduces the saving mentality early:** The child develops a strong saving mentality when they learn early in life what saving is and how to do it. Saving becomes a part of their financial habit rather than something they struggle with even as adults.

- **Builds discipline and self-control:** A child who learns to save early in life develops a strong sense of self-control and discipline, a critical part of building wealth. The child learns early in life that they do not need to purchase every new shiny thing; they do not need to spend all the money in their pocket, and this discipline is what puts them on the path to building wealth in the future.

- **Self-dependency**: Children who develop a saving habit become self-dependent earlier in life because their savings help them make some purchases out of their pockets instead of always depending on you for everything. The savings can also help them buy themselves desired gadgets that you do not want to buy for them, such as a gaming console. If they save enough to make the purchase, they will care more for it because it will be bought from their hard-earned money, further making them appreciate the value of money.

- **Helps in emergency purposes**: Having savings also teaches a child that they will need the money for emergency purposes. For example, if they accidentally break a friend's toy, they can replace it using part of their savings. Or, if they need to make a certain purchase but you aren't around, they can use their savings to make the purchase, and you will then refund them the amount.

The Power of a Dollar a Day

One of the key philosophies of wealth building is keeping away a dollar each day. Sure, when we look at the bigger picture, this doesn't seem like much, but the focus should be less on the amount and more on the philosophy.

Teaching a child to save a dollar a day is teaching them a saving culture that will help them learn how to keep away a small amount of money each day for the future. It will also let them know that no amount of money is too small to become useful when the time is right.

But for example, if your child manages to keep a dollar away each day in a year, that would come to about $365 a year. To a child, this amount of money is quite transformative. It is enough money to buy a refurbished Apple iPhone 11 64 GB from Amazon while having some pocket change to buy Earpods.

But if you cannot give your child a dollar a day for allowance, you can still teach them this philosophy with any amount. You want them to understand that it is very possible to take care of your expenses while still putting aside money for other projects they may have. When they learn this early, they are in a great position to implement this idea with much more money in the future.

And to encourage them to save even more, below are some simple sayings that you can use to reinforce the savings culture in your children.

Simple Sayings, Simple Savings

Below are some simple sayings you can have printed out and stuck somewhere where they see it frequently, like on their study desk or their bedside drawer:

- ✓ *A dollar a day keeps the rainy days away* – **Unknown**

- ✓ *Never spend your money before you have it* – **Thomas Jefferson**

- ✓ *Do not save what is left after spending, but spend what is left after saving* – **Warren Buffett**

- ✓ *A budget is telling your money where to go, instead of wondering where it went* – **John C. Maxwell**

- ✓ *It is never too early to encourage long-term savings* – **Ron Lewis**

- ✓ *The habit of saving is itself an education. It fosters every virtue, teaches self-denial, cultivates the sense of order, trains for forethought, and so broadens the mind.* – **T.T Munger**

- *A man who both spends and saves money is the happiest because he has both enjoyment* – **Samuel Johnson.**

- *Save when you don't need it, and it'll be there for you when you do* – **Frank Sonnenberg.**

- *Saving is the foremost financial education we need, not finance* – **John Joclebs Bassey.**

- *It is not how much money you make, but how much money you keep, how hard it works for you, and how many generations you keep it for* – **Robert Kiyosaki.**

- *You must gain control over your money, or the lack of it will forever control you* – **Dave Ramsey.**

- *Being a smart shopper is the first step to getting rich* – **Mark Cuban**

- *It is thrifty to prepare today for the wants of tomorrow* – **Aesop**

- *Save money on the big, boring stuff so that you have something left over for life's simple pleasures* – **Elisabeth Leamy**

- ✓ *Small amounts saved daily add up to huge investments in the end* – **Margo Vader**

- ✓ *A simple fact that is hard to learn is that the time to save money is when you have some.* – **Joe Moore**

- ✓ *A wise person should have money in their head, but not in their heart.* – **Jonathan Swift**

Looking at these simple quotes will help remind the child that they are doing something right, and as they continue with that habit, they will find fulfillment in the future when they need their savings to do whatever they desire at that time in their lives.

Chapter 5: Understanding Expenses

"Beware of little expenses. A small leak will sink a great ship."

Benjamin Franklin

When building wealth, understanding expenses and how they influence every financial decision we make is crucial, and you want your child to be aware of this and make all the right choices.

In my experience, I do not think there is any one person who has built wealth by completely neglecting their expenses.

But first, what are expenses, and how do you define them to your child?

What are Expenses?

Sit your child down and ask them what they want to spend their money on. You can give them a pen and a paper to help them with the process.

Let them write down without interruption, and please encourage them to be free about what they desire most to spend their money on.

Then, once the child has these written down, please pick up the list and inform them that expenses are everything they have written down. So, an expense is anything we spend our money on. Make sure the child understands this.

Categorizing Expenses

With all that written down, together with the child, engage in a simple sorting activity where you categorize the expenses based on necessities and non-essentials.

You can do this on a different piece of paper or a different notebook page. Once again, to make the lesson stick, use color coding. For example, red can be for essentials, while black or any other neutral color can be for non-essential.

In essence, let them know that food and clothing items are part of essential expenses; these expenses will often be recurring and necessary for everyday life. These expenses will often take up a lot of their money, but that is okay because they would not live comfortably without them.

Then, for non-essentials, include expenses such as money spent on toys, candy, or entertainment. These expenses are non-essential because the child can live comfortably and happily without them, even if they might feel like they are going crazy because they don't have the latest gadget or toy to play with.

Here, you can use role-playing games to teach them the concept of wants vs needs. For example, provide a hypothetical sum of money and let them know they can spend it at will. Then, give them several options for expenses from the list they wrote. However, change them up a little bit to make it a little challenging. Here is an example:

1. They could use that money to buy a new pair of clothes.

2. They could use that money to buy a costly, unique gadget or toy they have always wanted.

3. They could use the money to buy ice cream and chocolate cakes they crave.

4. They could use the money to buy an air ticket to vacation in an exotic location.

5. They could use the money to pay for tuition fees.

Then, ask them to write down how they would spend the money based on their priorities. The aim is to teach the child to separate and differentiate between needs and wants.

Please do not interfere with them writing down the list. Let them write down the list based on their perception of that age. In fact, you could even step out and let them write down what they think will be a priority to use the money for.

Once done, go through the list and see how they did. Give them a score based on how well they have listed it based on needs vs wants. I know you might think, *'But won't it depend on different people?'* I do not think so.

No matter who you are, buying clothes and paying tuition fees are two very important priorities. They are needs you must put at the top of your mind before thinking of anything else; that is how the child should list them.

Let the child know that needs are expenses they must meet to live a comfortable and happy life. Buying clothes helps one cover themselves and look presentable everywhere they go, while paying tuition fees means they have access to education, a fundamental need for any self-respecting human being.

Now, if the child is younger, they might list ice cream and chocolate as a priority too, since, to a child, these are food, but also make sure they understand the difference between proper food and dessert or snacks.

While ice cream and chocolate are technically food, they are not the type of food we need to live a healthy life. Let them understand that the kinds of food that are a priority include food items such as cereals, vegetables, meat, milk, water, and bread.

Since these foods are rich in nutrients that the human body needs, they are a priority. Sugary snacks such as cakes and ice cream are wants because they merely pleasure our taste buds occasionally but are not necessary for our lives.

Now, this, of course, should not mean that the child cannot spend money on them. Let them know that they can spend money on ice cream and cake. However, it should only be after they have fulfilled all their essential needs.

When the child learns about what needs and wants are, they learn how to prioritize, which, unfortunately, most people lack.

Of course, here is where the rest of us differ from the rich people. Due to the vastness of their resources and the fact that they can do so, rich people will often take care of their wants and needs simultaneously. A rich person may buy a new, expensive gadget or toy as they buy food.

They might also decide to buy ice cream as they buy vegetables. Let the child know that this is because they can do so, which makes them different.

As for the rest of us, we need to set our priorities in order first, then spend the remaining amount on wants. Thus, they should not compare their situation to that of a rich person, whether it is another rich child they know of or whether they are trying to compare them to neighbors.

Importance of Delayed Gratification

Children will often not understand the concept of delayed gratification and often desire what they want at that moment and not in the future. Thus, you will need to take the initiative in teaching the lessons on delayed gratification so they also learn not to give in to their finance-related impulses instantly.

For example, let us say that the child is craving some ice cream. However, dinner is almost ready. As a parent, sit the child down and explain that they can have ice cream only after eating and finishing their dinner.

If the child is older, perhaps a teen, they could want a new gadget. Rather than letting them have it instantly, teach them the value of patience. Perhaps you could have them perform extra chores for a given amount of time before you can buy them the gadget.

When you teach children these lessons, they learn the value of delayed gratification, and this lesson will transfer into their finances when they are adults. After all, as the saying goes, *'Good things come to those who wait.'*

This lesson will also come in handy as they decide how to spend their pocket money. When you teach them to delay gratification, they will also begin to avoid spending their pocket money at the slightest opportunity they get.

Instead, they will begin to understand how much joy comes from delaying what you desire for a short while longer, perhaps to save more to buy something better or simply to wait for the right time to make the purchase, thus saving up on some money.

For example, they could wait for their favorite toy or gadget to go on sale and buy it at a discount. Not only will this mean they get their favorite toy after delaying the purchase and thus building the anticipation, but they also save some money – all because they chose to wait.

Delayed gratification is one of the core tenets of building wealth because it means one does not spend money at every instant they feel like it. That, then, allows them to save up the money they could otherwise have spent in an instant and spend it in the future on something bigger, better, or more useful. Or perhaps spend less money on an item and thus save up the remainder of the cost.

Expenses are a part of life, and they are often the things that will eat up a lot of the money we make. However, when you teach your child to prioritize very early, you give them a head start in learning to save and budget their money.

When the child learns the value of sorting out their essentials first, they are halfway through their saving process because it is often the essentials that people ignore that often come back to bite them right in their pockets.

But when your child is knowledgeable about this, they will take care of their core expenses and can then decide which non-essential they want to spend money on as they also save. And saving becomes a lot easier when we have covered all our core essentials.

Chapter 6: Unconventional Wisdom on Chores: Lessons on Building Wealth from Chores

"Every child must have chores to do. It gives them dignity in work and the joy of labor."

Earl Hamner Jr.

Doing chores is a part of growing up, or at least for all of us from poor households. Chores are often where we learn how to clean up after ourselves. It is where, if we are lucky enough, we earn our first allowance and can purchase what we desire at that age.

But if you are going to teach your child how to build wealth, then you are going to need to change how you teach them about chores and how they, in turn, interpret how they do their chores.

After teaching their children how to do chores for the first time, many parents often leave them to their own devices. They might step in to supervise them from time to time, but for the most part, the child will often be alone.

But if you want to teach your child about building wealth, you must get creative with how you teach them about chores. By reimagining the role chores play in your child's life, you will reveal hidden lessons that will be key in your child's journey to becoming financially literate.

While we might look at building wealth solely through earning, saving, and budgeting, financial wellness and health are also rooted in daily habits, habits whose lessons we can find in chores.

Chores Are More Than Just Chores

Chores often look like mundane things we do just so we can get through them quickly and move on to other bigger and better things. But there could be many more life skills we can distill and instill in our children through house chores.

Below are some lessons you can teach your child through house chores, which can then come in handy in helping them in their financial journey.

Learning Responsibility

House chores are perhaps among the most repetitive tasks anyone can ever do. They will often be never-ending, sometimes even needing you to perform them several times a day.

For example, washing dishes can sometimes need to be done twice or more times a day. Depending on the number of people in a household, laundry day can be once, twice, or even more times a week.

Thus, because these tasks are repetitive, it is very easy to get caught up in simply doing them on autopilot without thinking about what and how we should do them.

But house chores are a great place to teach your child responsibility. Through the commitment to doing the tasks each day, let the child know that they are slowly building the character needed to be a responsible, grown adult who doesn't sit around and wait for someone else to do everything for them.

When they learn to be responsible in this manner, this sense of responsibility will extend into their daily life as adults when they always need to be responsible for their actions, including how they spend their money.

Now, I know what you are thinking. *'How is there a link between doing chores and being responsible for how we spend money?'*

When children learn early in life how to do dishes and take responsibility and say, *'Let me do the dishes now rather than wait for someone else,'* they are learning how to take the initiative and not just wait for someone else to do it. Taking the initiative is a key part of achieving success in various aspects of life.

So, do not look for a direct link between doing house chores and earning money, though that is still possible. Rather, look at the lessons they might learn through doing chores.

Time Management

Another critical lesson children learn from doing house chores is time management.

Let me explain. Let us say your child wants to go out and meet friends at 3 PM, but they should also complete some house chores around the house before they can go and meet their friends.

Out of knowing that they should finish the house chores before leaving, the child will learn how to complete their assigned house chores at a designated time before stepping out of the house. This understanding of time and how to manage it is critical to future success because it is how the very successful among us do it.

Having spent some time around some wealthy folks, I have learned that they will often be very unhappy when someone wastes or attempts to waste their time. Whenever something needs completion at a given time, that is when it needs to be done.

When they want you to meet them at a given time, that is when you should meet them. Because they have such strict time management, is it a wonder that they have enough time left to continue building their wealth?

And time management is something that one is never too young to learn. But your child won't magically learn this lesson on their own. You must instill that sense of discipline in them so they build upon it on their own.

Let them know that if they stay committed to their chores, they leave a lot of free time to do other things. The value of doing something at its designated time helps them avoid being held back by the chores at a time when they should be doing something else.

Additionally, incentivize them each time they complete a task on time so they can continually do it. For example, you can give them some extra playing time each time they complete a task on time.

By rewarding their persistent efforts to stay on time, you encourage them to be doing the tasks on time.

Conversely, they can lose some of those privileges if they take too long to complete a task. This way, you disincentivize the lack of time management through negative reinforcement. The next time they go to do a task, they will have it at the back of their mind that they have a lot to lose if they don't complete it on time.

Builds Work Ethic

I know you might be asking how. As mentioned earlier in this chapter, house chores will often be repetitive; many recur daily or once every two or three days.

Thus, for one to continue to do house chores without feeling the need to give up, they need to be committed to the task at hand, and that commitment is what it means to have a strong work ethic.

When you teach the child that staying committed to doing their house chores helps them build a strong work ethic, you are also helping them build a key part of what will make them successful in their adult lives.

You see, wealth and success are built on that commitment to what you are doing, that ability to continue down the path toward success even if it seems boring, mundane, and repetitive.

Someone committed to their work, someone who wakes up daily and commits themselves to the habits that are bringing them success, is halfway through building wealth for themselves and their future generation.

And the lesson of such commitment is found in the mundanity of house chores. Teach the child to appreciate the fact that house chores teach them to stay committed to something, even when it becomes boring.

Liken the chores to other financial concepts. For example, their commitment to doing house chores daily even when they do not feel like it is what saving feels like. For example, completing a house task on time could be like going shopping and staying in the black once you have shopped for everything.

Let the child know that they will need such deep levels of commitment to their work or business in the future, even when they get bored by what might feel like a humdrum and boring existence.

But simply letting the child know the link between house chores and future financial literacy is not the whole step. To build that commitment, you must also find creative ways to encourage them to stay committed to the course.

Here is how:

Building the Spirit of Commitment Through Chores

Your child will need to see in real-time that their efforts are translating or at least will translate to what you tell them, so here is how to help them build that spirit of commitment through house chores.

Introduce Non-Monetary Rewards

Begin by recognizing your child's commitment to house chores by introducing non-monetary rewards each time they complete a task well and within the set timeline. Remember, right now, you want to build the spirit of commitment, not just teach them about financial benefits.

So, once they complete a task, acknowledge and praise them for completing the chores well and on time and let them know that this recognition is a valuable reward in and of itself.

When they do this persistently, offer them non-monetary privileges, such as extra playtime or extra time with friends if they are teenagers. Or they could be in charge of choosing a family activity as a reward for staying committed and putting in consistent effort to complete their house chores.

This way, you build their commitment to doing the activity, which earns them rewards, and this commitment will come in handy when dealing with their finances in the future.

Use Chores to Teach Them Goal-Setting

Letting your child know that chores are opportunities for them to learn about goal-setting is another great way to build that spirit of commitment.

Let us say that the chores are a lot, and they feel overwhelmed. Then, you could ask them to break the chores down into smaller tasks that they can then complete one after another.

For example, let's assume they should do laundry and perhaps clean the dishes. You can teach them to set a target to do laundry first, since it tends to be the heavier of the two tasks, and then come to do the dishes. And when doing the dishes, they can also break it further down into smaller tasks. They can begin cleaning the cups and spoons, then move on to cleaning the plates, and finally do the pots.

Through setting goals and breaking the chores into smaller tasks, the child learns a valuable lesson on how to make something big and impossible easily achievable. This lesson will come in handy in their financial journey.

For example, by breaking down their saving journey into smaller saving targets, they can save more and for bigger things.

Be There for Them Through It All

To further reinforce the lessons you are trying to teach, ensure you are there for them from time to time so that you provide consistent positive reinforcement for them to stay committed to the course.

Remember, even as your child grows and begins to live alone, they will still require your help as a parent, and you want them to know that the good behavior they display also has the reward of you listening to them.

Be there for them so you can address any challenges they encounter as they do their chores. Periodically check up on them as they do their chores so that you can help them out when they feel stuck.

Regularly listen to them and adapt your approach based on the child's desires and what aligns with their liking.

This way, the child learns to stay committed to the course because they know you are there to guide them through it all, thus incentivizing them to continue doing that given task.

Foster the Entrepreneurial Spirit Through Creativity

Did you know you can use house chores to foster the entrepreneurial spirit in your child? Entrepreneurship is all about creativity and innovation while still completing the task as intended.

Thus, encourage your child to approach the chores with creativity and innovation. Discuss how the child can find efficient ways to complete the tasks, which is akin to entrepreneurial problem-solving.

They don't need to come up with a complex solution immediately. A simple, creative way to efficiently clean the house chores is all they need. By finding solutions to common house chore problems, you are building that entrepreneurial spirit within them and, thus, putting them on the path to future financial success.

Please also encourage them to take the initiative from time to time in planning and organizing their chores how they want them organized. Doing this builds their confidence in their organizational skills and makes them understand how to take the initiative, which, as you know, are all traits of an entrepreneur.

Build The Intrinsic Motivation

Another way to build the spirit of commitment to the task is by encouraging them to focus on intrinsic motivation. As you know, staying committed to any journey requires demands that we find a sense of internal fulfillment that can keep us going.

Thus, share with the child the intrinsic rewards that come with completing tasks and chores on time. Let them know that the sense of accomplishment that comes with viewing a clean room or looking at a clean kitchen is a reward in and of itself, and thus, they should not focus solely on external rewards.

By shifting their focus internally, you also encourage them to focus on good, responsible behavior for deeper internal satisfaction rather than simply because there is an external reward. By focusing on internal satisfaction, they reinforce their commitment to good habits.

As they persistently stay committed to good behavior, they put themselves in a great position to show the same level of commitment to their financial goals and targets, even when that commitment does not have a direct reward.

As you can see, you can teach your child plenty of lessons about their future success and financial rewards through house chores. As a parent, when your child is old enough to shoulder the responsibility of house chores and complete them without supervision, then they are old enough to learn lessons you can teach them.

First, let them understand why doing house chores is more than just completing tasks. Let them know that they are learning responsibility and time management and that this builds their work ethics, all three qualities they will need in their adult lives when building their wealth.

Then, after teaching these lessons, begin using the house chores to build their commitment spirit. Make the tasks a place where they can learn goal-setting, a place where they can build their entrepreneurial spirit, and where they can build that sense of fulfillment beyond external motivation.

With time, house chores will go from simple, mundane everyday tasks to opportunities for your child to build habits that will help them in their financial journey in the future.

Chapter 7: Dreaming Big: Being Unlimited in Thoughts and Action

> *"I would say always follow your dream. And dream big because my whole career, including any of the things I've accomplished, I never thought in a million years I would be here. So it just proves that once you believe in yourself, and you put your mind to something, you can do it."*
>
> *Simone Biles*

There is a saying I often find very encouraging that pushes one to be greater than they currently are: *If your dreams are not scaring you, then they are not big enough.*

This quote is straightforward, but it also resonated deeply with my soul because it forms the basis of the lesson you should teach your child about finances.

Before getting into the lesson of this chapter about dreaming big, allow me to share a story that represents why dreaming big matters.

If you know your Hollywood stars, then I am certain you know Jim Carrey. Carrey is one of the most successful and revered actors of all time, well-known for his great sense of humor.

Many do not know that Jim Carrey grew up in a poor household, and if his acting career hadn't panned out, he said he would be working at a steel factory in Ontario.

Early in his career, Jim Carrey struggled to find work and progress his career in the entertainment industry. His father supported his dreams and would drive him to perform at comedy clubs.

However, for the most part, his performances, which involved impersonations, would bomb, which increased Carey's doubts about his future. Back home, with each failure, it became difficult for his family to support his ambitions.

But Jim Carrey had a big dream, and he believed in himself to achieve it. So, in 1985, Carrey made an daring decision to write himself a $10 million check for 'acting services rendered.' He dated that check 10 years into the future and kept it in his wallet.

Fast forward to 10 years later, in November 1995, Carrey would be cast in his breakout role in the movie Dumb and Dumber in Hollywood. His pay for that movie was 10 million dollars!

Now, this was someone who had nothing as he was writing himself that check but believed that someday in the future, he would have that money. That is what dreaming big does: it allows you to have a strong belief in yourself and then make the choices you believe will get you there.

That is a very important story to share with your child to teach them the value of self-belief and having big dreams that scare them.

Why Having Big Dreams Matters in Building Wealth

Now, if we look back at Jim Carrey's story, we can call it whatever we want: coincidence, the law of attraction, or the power of self-belief. Whatever you call it, the lesson here is that when you dream big enough and believe in yourself enough, you will achieve it.

Thus, let the child know that having big dreams is great for building wealth because it does the following:

- **It excites them:** Let's be honest here as parents: big dreams are exciting. When your kids have big dreams, they will feel excited about achieving them, especially if, beyond motivating them to have big dreams, you also play your role right and show them how to turn those big dreams into actionable milestones they can work towards each passing day. Excitement is an important ingredient in wealth-building because it makes kids more willing to apply the money lessons you teach them. It also makes them passionate about what their financial training and goals.

- **Pushes them outside their comfort zone**: Building wealth never happens when one is within their comfort zone. People have left their home countries behind to build wealth. Others have learned new skills so that they can build wealth. Thus, let the child know that when they have big dreams that scare them, these dreams help push them beyond their comfort zone and, thus, put them on the path to wealth creation.

- **Gives them something to work towards**: Let the child know that it is not enough to want to build wealth. Let them dream big about what they want to do when they achieve that wealth. Would it be to ensure their family doesn't struggle in life again? Would it be to help their community? Would it be to finally achieve the financial freedom to buy whatever they have always desired? Whatever it is, let the child know that having a big dream of what they want to do with their wealth helps them in their wealth creation journey.

- **Forces them to make good financial decisions**: Having money without knowing how and where you would like to use it is a very dangerous combination. Having a dream or something to work towards, such as wealth creation for posterity, helps the child make better financial decisions because they have a lot riding on it. Whether the decision seems small, like cutting back excess expenditure, or as big as seeking a better job, they will make better financial decisions if they have a dream.

- **Teaches them perseverance**: Jim Carrey waited 10 years for his big dream to come true. Even then, it was still not guaranteed, but that only made him push himself further without giving up. The same is true if your child has big dreams about what they want to do when they grow up. When they dream big, they develop perseverance, which means they will remain steadfast in their march toward their dream without ever giving up because they strongly believe in their ability to bring their dreams to fruition.

- **Sets them up for success**: You've heard it said that if you can dream it, you can have it. It's true; every great achievement that humankind has ever achieved started with a dream in someone's mind and heart. That's why you should motivate your kids to dream big: their dreams could be the next life-changing innovation or business idea. Additionally, motivating kids to dream as big as possible is a great way to set them up for success because achieving big dreams requires a lot of learning and re-learning. For example, kids with big dreams must also learn essential skills like time management, taking action, a positive attitude, breaking big goals into smaller milestones, etc. Learning these skills can be like a ladder to success.

Dreaming big and building wealth are two peas in a pod; thus, you should encourage your child to let their imagination run wild because it is the best way to build the confidence they need to achieve what they set out to achieve.

So, how do you teach them this?

How To Help Kids Dream Big

Dreaming big is not something your child will begin to do once you share with them the importance or benefits of dreaming big. You must also put in the hard yards so they learn it from practical experience.

Here is how to do that:

Encourage Them to Write It Down

Jim Carrey wrote himself a $10 million check at a point in time when his career was in the doldrums, and this helped him a lot in the choices he made in the coming ten years.

Writing down their big dreams helps kids make great choices from then on. And this isn't something made up.

According to Sir John Hargrave, CEO of the communication company Media Shower, in his book *Mind Hacking*, writing down our ideas, thoughts, and resolutions is a game-changer.

According to Hargrave, writing is a *"gateway behind the world of mind and the world of matter."* Writing transforms thoughts into things, and we get ideas from inside our heads into our hands.

His observation resonates in a 2008 study funded by the National Institute of Health. The study recruited 1,700 people to lose weight by keeping a food diary of what they ate.

The results found that the more records people kept records of what they ate, the more weight they lost. Knowing they had recorded their food choices rather than eating and forgetting about them became a powerful motivator to make better choices.

These two examples show us the power of simply writing down something.

Thus, please encourage your child to write down the goals they hope to achieve as adults. These goals will help them make better choices throughout the next years and will lead them toward their set aims and goals.

And encourage them to write down their biggest dream. Please encourage them to write down that dream about building a multi-million-dollar business, about becoming top professionals in the field they desire, and about becoming wealthy.

That helps them build the confidence to go after it and make choices that lead them towards it.

Champion Their Passion

Jim Carrey's check story would not have been such a success had his family not put in the efforts they did to support him early on in his career. His father had fully invested and dedicated himself to driving him to comedy clubs even though his son's shows often failed. Still, Jim's father kept the faith in him.

This belief from his father is possibly another part of why Jim Carrey felt confident in himself to the extent of writing that check.

Thus, please foster an environment where your child's dreams and desires feel valued. Whatever they write down as their biggest dream, you should create an enabling environment for them to pursue it.

If your child dreams of building wealth by starting a business, encourage them to be specific about what kind of business they want to start, and then find out how you can support them through it all. Buy them books from business people in the area of specialization they want or other big dreamers such as Martin Luther King or Harriet Tubman.

Take them to conferences to listen to their favorite successful person or people and allow them to network and ask questions about whatever industry they want to enter as adults.

Championing their passion also means equipping them with the tools they need to succeed in their chosen field.

Whether that is enrolling them in a business class if they want to get into business or funding their education to the level required for them to succeed in the field they desire.

Whatever additional skill they need for that particular field, please support them in it.

Let Them Make Mistakes

Mistakes pave the journey to building wealth. The difference between those who succeed and those who don't is usually how each responds to the mistakes they make.

Many parents often feel that, since their child has an idea of what they want or now that they are teaching them building wealth techniques, then they should not be making mistakes. But that is not how it works.

If anything, you should be prepared for many mistakes from your child since this is technically unchartered territory. They are dreaming about building wealth from scratch – mistakes in this instant are bound to be many,

If you want your child to dream big and continue dreaming big, then let them make mistakes. Please encourage them to be daring and to do things beyond their comfort zone. Be a champion for making mistakes.

Teach them the lesson that making mistakes is nothing to be ashamed of. Every wealthy person, every successful person they see, including those they admire, made mistakes several times. So, they should not be too hard on themselves after making mistakes.

Once they make a mistake, they should see that as a lesson on what not to do in their journey towards achieving their dreams rather than a failing on their part.

By embracing their mistakes and using them as stepping stones for bigger and better things, they gain the confidence to keep believing in themselves and what they want to achieve.

Give Them Their Free Time

While you are funding their dreams and helping them move toward their big dreams, also allow them their free time. Pre-teens and teens are often old enough to want you to give them the freedom to do some soul-searching and self-discovery.

Thus, if your child doesn't seem to have any particular big dream or know what they hope to do to build wealth, do not be all up in their business or personal space trying to push them in a certain direction. That will only result in them rebelling against you, thus breaking any hopes of you teaching them further lessons.

Hold space for them to try out different activities, have different dreams, and discover their passions. Remember, this age is for self-discovery; thus, they should feel free to explore the various parts of themselves.

And even if the child seems to have a set dream or goal, encourage them to continue trying various other things. If they find something they feel could be valuable to them in the future, encourage them to pursue it without feeling like they need to stick to one thing only.

Remember, the people who build massive wealth usually also have various income streams. Therefore, the more skills and knowledge your child has, the more chances they have to put themselves on the path to success.

Thus, please encourage your children to have a big dream of building wealth but encourage them to pursue different fields they can use to get there. They shouldn't limit themselves to just one path.

Building wealth requires that one is not limited in one's beliefs and dreams. Once someone can dream big and believe their desire is well within reach, they are well on their way to building wealth.

By encouraging the child to pursue their passion through supporting them in the various things they do in their childhood, you are opening up the path for them to build wealth in the future.

But, even as they learn to dream big, it is important that they also learn that money moves fast, and they need special skills to manage the money they will get.

Chapter 8: Homeschool Money and Life Skills

"Education must not simply teach work - it must teach Life."

W. E. B. Du Bois

For many of us, homeschooling often seems like a foreign concept, especially if, like me, you grew up outside the U.S., where this concept is not widespread.

However, since moving to the U.S., I have become familiar with the homeschooling concept and learned that home-based learning can be a vital intersection of education and financial training. Think about it.

When you homeschool your child, you decide the lessons they will learn. Here in the U.S., there is no legal requirement for a child to follow the curriculum in U.S. schools when homeschooling. The only strict requirement is that your child learn well and regularly to the standards set in school.

Thus, as the person in charge of the curriculum, why would you not want to introduce financial lessons and life skills to them as they learn?

I have met many parents who homeschool their children and will often include some more extra-curricular activities, such as taekwondo, or practical skills, such as DIY. Still, very few often think of introducing financial and life skills to their children.

Yet finances are one of the critical parts of our lives because they shape how we evolve through the years until we die. So, why would such a skill not be mandatory for children to learn?

The Advantage of Homeschooling in Finances

Homeschooling provides a unique and intimate environment for instilling financial literacy in children. As a parent, there are several advantages that homeschooling provides when teaching your child about money, and they are:

- **Your child learns about money from someone they trust**: The topic of money is a very touchy one, even for children. Thus, when you take it upon yourself to be the one who homeschools your child, you create an environment where the child feels freer because they are learning about finances from someone they trust.

- **The home creates an enabling environment for practical lessons:** I am sure if your child goes to school and learns about finances, most of it will be theory because, for the most part, the teacher will not have the time for personalized teaching lessons since they have many students to teach.

  However, as a parent homeschooling your child, you have the time and resources to give your child more personalized teachings and practical lessons. For example, when teaching them about money management, you can give them real-life money and a hypothetical scenario where they need to use it and have them break down how to use it practically.

- **Homeschooling takes in the child's unique style, learning pace, and interests:** Many of us underestimate just how much personality and interests play a part in our financial habits. It might seem trivial, but learning about finances in a way that suits your personality matters a lot, and homeschooling provides this opportunity for your child.

  When you decide to homeschool your child and introduce them to financial literacy, you will tailor your lessons in ways that account for your child's personality, interests, and learning pace. You will tailor lessons that cater individually to them rather than provide them with generic and vague lessons.

- **You teach your child finances as you desire:** Your child learning about finances from someone else will often be a very big risk due to the different upbringing many of us have had.

  However, when you homeschool your child and decide to teach them about finances, you are in charge of the lessons you want and, thus, can make them view finances in a way you would want them to view it.

When the child learns about finances in a way they enjoy, the lessons will stick better, and they will make better financial decisions without feeling like they are betraying their true self.

But seeing these advantages, what financial lessons can you teach kids through homeschooling?

Financial Lessons to Teach Your Child in Homeschooling

Here are various such lessons:

Counting Money

I know that much of the world is going digital, and there is a lot of talk about digital currency replacing physical money, but at this point, counting real money remains a vital life skill.

Have you ever found yourself in a situation where you need to count a significant sum of money and find it hard to do it? That's because you did not learn the valuable skill of counting money fast and effectively. You wouldn't want your child to go through this in the future now, would you?

Counting money is a foundational skill that often requires basic arithmetic skills and some talent.

Use practical lessons by giving your child a stash of $1 bills and asking them to count them. Depending on the sum, set a timer. Ensure they know how to count the money without needing to extract the bills and put them on the desk or table.

"When you put money on the table when counting, you risk losing it, either through getting stolen or the wind blowing it away." Tell them this so they know how to count money while keeping it in their hands.

Another important skill is teaching them to sort the money based on denominations. Give them different U.S paper currency denominations mixed up and ask them to sort through them and arrange them in their respective denominations and then give you the total. Time them on this exercise, too.

Once again, this might seem like a fruitless lesson as money is going digital. However, having spoken to many people, most people still have a widespread desire to hold, interact with, and have physical money with them, whether in their wallets or purses. So, physical money is not going completely extinct any time soon. Let the child learn how to handle and count them.

Taxes and Tax Forms

Some adults often joke that they struggle with taxes because they never learned these lessons as kids. But the joke highlights a serious issue: the severe knowledge gap between most adults and their ability to pay taxes.

I have struggled to pay my taxes previously and had to learn about the steps as an adult, but you don't have to wait for your child to grow to teach them how to do this.

It pays to introduce them to the concept of taxes as soon as possible, probably as they get into high school. Perhaps they might have learned about what a tax is at school, but now, it is up to you to teach them more about it in depth.

For example, let them know that they will be required to file their taxes for each income they earn, and failure to do so will result in penalties. Let them know that the penalties will often accrue over time, and thus, when they get the invoice to pay it, it will pose a significant financial burden to them, thus affecting their ability to save or invest.

When filing your income tax, let them sit with you and watch you make the calculations on the Form 1040 that you file. Take them through the various parts of the form you are filing.

For example, form 1040 is the U.S. Individual Income Tax Return form and is the starting point for all taxpayers. That is the form your child will most likely fill after going into employment, self-employment, or when reporting income based on the sale of property. So, teach them about it for starters.

I know you may not understand the whole of it yourself, but try to answer their questions as best as you can. Also, explain the different IRS forms besides Form 1040 while at it. Many adults do not know the different forms and their use, but you can still give your child a heads up in this department so that they are not completely lost when it comes time to file their taxes.

That will be a challenging lesson to teach, but it will be a very important one that will help your child escape penalties on their money when they could be saving or investing. It will also help them escape court cases for tax fraud, which will often take up valuable time they could have spent earning more income.

Profits, Losses and Revenue

Even if your child isn't keen on getting into business, they must understand the dynamics of financial transactions. Thus, they need to understand the concept of profit, losses, and revenue in business.

I don't know about you, but I have met and interacted with many people who, at one point or another in their lives, got into business. Thus, even if your child has no interest in business, teaching them about profit, losses, and revenue will still come in handy for that period in their adult years when they consider it because it seems like a rite of passage at this rate.

Through simple, easy-to-teach lessons, you can easily teach them these three concepts. If you run a business, this lesson will be easier to teach because you will explain the concepts to them through your business.

Here is an example of how you can go about teaching them this concept:

You can have a board on which you explain your business to them. Then, write down how much your business makes in sales in a year (these don't have to be real figures). Then, ask them what the money represents.

For many children, that money will be the profit. And here is where you correct them and let them know that the money is not the profit but total revenue.

Teach them that revenue is the total amount a business makes from all its sales in a year. Let them know that a profit is the amount of money a business has left once it has covered all the costs of running a business. So, in this instance, you teach them the subtractions you would make from that total revenue, such as overhead costs—rent, water, and electricity bills— paying suppliers and settling other debts, and paying employee salaries if you have any. The money left after doing all that is the profit.

On loss, let them know that if, after you deduct costs from your revenue, the subtractions are more than the revenue, then the business has suffered a loss despite making a lot in revenue.

That is also where lessons of being in the red and being in the black come in handy. Let them know that when your business makes a profit, it is in the black. That means there is enough money left for other ventures aside from taking care of business expenses, just like when they have enough money left with them after making a purchase, they are also in the black.

When a business makes a loss, that is, when the cost of subtractions exceeds the revenue, then the business is in the red. Thus, there is not enough money for other expenditures, just like how they are in the red when they spend all of their pocket money to make a purchase and need to borrow some more to settle the remaining cost.

Let them understand that while a loss is not the goal, a business can continue operating after making a loss. However, if it keeps making losses a lot more frequently than it turns a profit, then that business is failing since it's not making money.

You can give them an example: if they keep spending their pocket money without adding more savings or getting any more allowances, they will soon deplete the money.

Negotiation Skills

Another important part of financial literacy is learning how to negotiate. I don't know about you, but I consider negotiating a key skill when seeking not just how you want to spend money but also how you want to earn it.

I am specifically looking at bargaining skills that your child needs to learn early in life so that nobody takes advantage of them by charging them more for a product or service than it is worth.

Here, you can give the child many more practical lessons. Have them accompany you to a place where you make a purchase. Make sure it is a place where bargaining is acceptable. Then, ask them to observe how you reason with the seller for the best price possible for a product or service.

Let them observe how you navigate the dispute until you agree.

When desiring to save money and create ideal conditions for building wealth, then being able to bargain and get the best deals when making a purchase is important. If rich people can bargain, why won't the rest of us?

Once they have accompanied you in a few of these practical lessons, then give them some money and have them go to make a purchase. Accompany them the first few times and see how they bargain.

This process helps them put into practice their bargaining skills while also helping them build the confidence to be able to state their price assertively so they can get a fair price and save some bucks.

When you teach them negotiation skills, they will come in handy when making purchases and when they want to negotiate a fair salary or wage wherever they will be working.

While growing up, many of us learned to believe that once a prospective employer sets a salary, that is it. However, it is absolutely possible to negotiate for higher and better pay with a prospective employer based on skills, job experience, and education level.

When your child develops their negotiation skills early, they become much more skilled at the practice. They will also be confident enough to negotiate for better pay before getting employed or for a pay rise once they are already employed.

When looking at homeschooling your child based on what we have discussed in this chapter, an overarching theme emerges: homeschooling is not merely an alternative to traditional education. It is a dynamic platform on which you can nurture a vibrant, all-rounded human being, including a financially savvy individual.

By embracing the endless possibilities homeschooling accords, especially the advantages it gives you in teaching financial matters, parents can equip their children with practical life skills that extend far beyond the realms of academic and financial skills that they might otherwise not have been able to learn in school.

Whether the skill is counting money, understanding profit and loss, understanding taxes and the different tax forms, or developing real-life money-saving skills such as negotiating, parents can become the architects of a comprehensive financial education for their children.

Homeschooling is an opportunity to shape a child's academic knowledge and foundational understanding of money. This skill will undoubtedly serve them well on their financial literacy and success journey.

Chapter 9: Building a Long-Term Perspective on Financial Decisions

"We must shift our thinking away from short-term gain toward long-term investment and sustainability and always have the next generations in mind with every decision we make."

Deb Haaland

Many of us make financial decisions based on a few short-term things we often want to do and feel the need to do immediately. The temptation of making money and then spending it like it is going out of fashion is hardly a new phenomenon.

For ages, many people have struggled with developing a long-term perspective when making financial decisions, only to find themselves unwillingly back to being penniless once their income stream dries up.

I remember hearing a story about two friends who decided to go on a trip to celebrate their friendship. The two friends were James and Frank.

Now, James was a very high-earning individual. He was in the tech industry and was working for a major tech corporation. He was one of the very low-ranked employees at the company but was still well-remunerated.

His salary was, in fact, a lot more than that of his friend, Frank. Frank wasn't earning peanut, but compared to James, he might as well have. Thus, putting together money for this trip took him some time, so when they took the trip, he had a budget and a detailed spending plan to help him with how he would spend his money.

Once they got to their holiday destination, they went about enjoying their holiday. James was a lot more generous with how he spent his money, and he often spent it on impulse. The two would be walking down the street, and James would see something he liked and, without thinking twice, would fish out his card or cash in his pockets and purchase it.

The problem was that James often spent most of the money on things they would use instantly: drinks, snacks, and whatnot.

On the other hand, Frank, while not exactly miserly either, was a lot more frugal. After all, he was on holiday, so he needed to use the money to enjoy himself. However, he tried spending his money more wisely.

He purchased items that would not only remind him of his trip in the long term but also items that he thought would be of value when he got back home. He also managed to buy some items for his house, which he found at cheaper prices at their holiday destination.

After getting back home, the two then went their respective ways. The two met for lunch a few days later, but James did not seem happy. When Frank asked him what was wrong, James scratched his head ruefully.

"I feel as though the trip has just disappeared from my memory like that," he said. *"I have nothing to show for it. I know I have the memories, but the trip still doesn't feel real. It almost feels like a fever dream."*

On the other hand, Frank had no such problems. On top of the memories of the trip, he also had souvenirs that reminded him of his time during the holiday. He could pinpoint exactly where he was when he bought a certain item, which made the memories of the trip even more real.

The story above exemplifies what happens when one spends money with a short-term vision vs what happens when one does so with a long-term vision.

When teaching your children finances, you want them to understand that spending money means they need to think long-term, irrespective of whether the purchase is as small as a packet of milk or as large as a car or home.

Each time they make the purchase, they should think, *'What are the long-term implications of this financial decision?'* And this attitude brings us to the topic many people do not seem to enjoy: investing.

Now, this book is not for you to teach your child about investing, but I felt we could not talk about building wealth and creating good financial habits without talking about investing.

Investing: Putting Long-Term Financial Thinking in Action

Investing is a finance topic that elicits different reactions from many people. For those like me who are not exactly Richie Rich, it is a topic we believe and feel barely applies to us.

But investing is more than just buying stocks or shares in a company or business. Investing is about spending money on something that you believe will bring you value in the future.

When your child spends some of their pocket money on buying a toy or a phone, that toy or phone is an investment because the purpose of buying it is to extract some value from it. Thus, because investing is something that applies to all of us, teaching your child how to make the right investment at that age is a great way of helping them learn how to spend money on something that brings them value in the long term.

How to Teach Your Child About Making a Long-Term Investment

Since we have established that any investment is anything we put money into while hoping to extract some value from it, teaching kids how to gauge a good or bad investment is critical.

Below are some skills you should teach your child to gauge whether an investment is good or bad:

Cost to benefit ratio

The first thing your child needs to understand is that when investing, they need to consider how much value they will extract from the investment based on the cost.

For example, if your child wants to buy a gadget, how costly is it, and for how long will it last? When investing, they need to learn that they should be able to extract maximum value from the product. A higher-cost product should give them more value over a longer period. They should also understand that quality should always precede quantity.

If they find a good quality product, but it is costly, they should consider purchasing it because a high-quality product will last them a very long time, thus saving them money in the long term. On the other hand, cheaper alternatives might save them some coins now, but because they are most likely poor quality, they will need to replace them frequently, thus spending more money in the long run.

For example, if the choice is buying a cheap plastic toy that they like and a costlier, good-quality toy, they should opt for the costlier quality toy even if it means spending a bit more than they intended. That way, they will not need to spend any future money they make on the same toy as the good-quality, costlier toy will last them for a longer time.

Meanwhile, they should not spend too much money on products that give them value for a very short time, even if the product is of a low cost. For example, candy might be very cheap, but they should not spend too much on it because, while it is cheap, its cost-to-benefit ratio over time is negative, meaning they will end up spending more money on candy than the benefits they get from it.

How much of their money should they use?

Your child should also know that spending all their money on an investment is unwise.

Let them know that when seeking to invest in something, they should aim to spend a certain percentage of their money on that investment. Sure, from time to time, they might need to spend all their savings on making a purchase, but for the most part, they should not spend all their money on an investment.

This lesson will teach them to be aware of their spending and not get too caught up in spending all their money simply because they feel or believe they can get great value for their money.

So, in this instance, you can play the key role of an investment adviser. You can tell the child that each time they want to buy something, they should come to you for advice on whether or not the item is worth the money they want to spend on it and how much of their money they should put in that investment.

Teach them about compounding

As you delve deeper into investing, you will need to get past the basic lessons on investing and teach them about compound interest. Let them know that aside from buying toys and gadgets, they can also put their money into an activity that can grow the money for them.

To make them understand compound interest, use the example of planting a seed. When they plant a seed into the ground and care for it by watering it and ensuring it gets enough sunlight, the seed will eventually grow into a tree tha will give them more seeds.

Thus, show them how the amount they put aside as savings (from the amount you give them as their allowance) could grow significantly over time.

Here, you could introduce them to investment accounts that yield compound interest. Explain to the child how, if they put a certain amount of money in such an account, the money will grow over time, giving them a bigger return on their money in the future.

This concept will be difficult to explain using toys or analogies, so please get creative. You could, for example, ask them to give you some part of their savings, which you get to keep in a separate piggy bank that you get to keep. Then, you can put pocket change in that account from time to time so that by the time you hand the piggy bank back to them, the initial money they gave you has grown significantly.

That is an oversimplification of what compounding is. Still, it is a very effective way of introducing the child to the basic idea of putting their money into an investment and letting it grow, even as they make other savings.

Lessons from Successful Investors

Successful investors are the people who drive world economies. People like Warren Buffet, Peter Lynch, the late Charlie Munger, Bill Miller, and Cathie Wood are some of the most successful investors in the world, and they all provide us with impeccable knowledge on how to invest and build wealth.

Below are some lessons you can teach your child about investing from successful investors.

They Are Not Too Young to Learn Investing

Warren Buffet was born to congressman and businessman Howard Buffet. That gave him an advantage when it came to developing an interest in business and investing, with Buffet buying his first stock at just 11 years old. He then delved into real estate at age 14, and from there, the rest is history.

The same is true for the late Peter Lynch. Born in 1944, Peter Lynch lost his father to cancer when he was just ten years old. To help his mother support their family, while barely in his teens, young Peter Lynch started working as a caddy. He soon began working at a high-scale upscale golf club.

While working there, he developed an interest in the stock market through overhearing conversations from the investors and business people who frequented the golf club.

While still in college, at around age 21 or 22, Peter Lynch made successfully invested in Flying Tiger, an air freight company. The money he earned from this investment helped him pay for graduate school.

So, if your child feels like they are too young to learn about investing, share Warren Buffet's and Peter Lynch's stories to encourage them that they have it in them to do it.

Let them know that their mind is the only thing stopping them from achieving their dreams of building wealth. Build their confidence so that, even if they do not invest in their childhood (many people are unlikely to invest in their childhood), they will still have this knowledge from very early in life, thus giving them an edge in whatever they choose to do in their adult lives.

Carving Their Own Path When Investing is Key

Bill Miller stands apart in the investing world because he often takes a different approach to investing. Bill Miller often foregoes traditional investing options in favor of investment based on his understanding of what he values in an investment.

For example, rather than investing in already well-established markets, he instead concentrates on undervalued stocks that have a great chance of future success.

The same is true for Cathie Wood, who, instead of prioritizing investing in already established companies, focuses her investment on small companies that she views as poised for exponential growth through technological advancement.

From this story, you can teach your child that they do not need to follow conventional investing wisdom. They can use their knowledge to map their path when investing.

Sure, they should pick lessons from all investors and take in the knowledge, but when it comes to putting their money where their mouth is, they should make the decision based on their understanding.

Wealth Building is a Gradual Process

The lesson we learn from all these investors is that they often invest their money with an eye for long-term gains over short-term, quick gains.

Many of these investors will often have no problems waiting for decades for their money to grow; thus, your child should know that if they choose to get into investing, they should think long-term. Let them know that, even if they start investing early in their life, they will still need to wait a while before seeing any substantial returns.

Thus, this is why they should learn about investing very early in life; the earlier they invest, the sooner they can make potential earnings from their investments.

Introduces Them to Strategic Thinking

Investing is all about strategy and tact; thus, let your children know they need to develop their strategic thinking early in life, especially if they want an edge.

By choosing long-term vision over short-term pressure, the most successful investors have built wealth beyond their wildest imagination, all thanks to strategic thinking. You could introduce them to this concept through the following example:

Let us say the child wants to make a purchase. However, the problem is they can't decide between two items. One of these items is, say, a very tasty piece of snack, while the other is a fruit. Which of these items would they be willing to buy and why?

When the child chooses, let them know why that choice is good or bad.

Let us say they choose the snack. Let them know that that was not strategic thinking because they chose a piece of food that was not very beneficial to their body. Instead, it was a food that won't positively affect their body.

Meanwhile, if they chose the fruit, they were choosing something that would have long-term benefits for their body. Thus, this displays strategic thinking because they thought of the long-term impact of the fruit on their overall health.

Through this simple example and many more that you will think of, your child will learn to develop a way of thinking where they strategically think of the long-term and short-term impacts of a financial decision before making it. That will be key in their journey to wealth building.

Investing is a major part of wealth building. That's why I felt it prudent to touch on it since you should do your best to introduce your child to the concept.

None of this means the child needs to invest that early in life. When we look at people who invested in their childhood or teens, many of them came from privileged backgrounds, something your child might not have.

Instead, focus on introducing your child to these concepts and ideas on investing. Give them practical investing examples and why they need to be wise about where they choose to put their money.

Share with them the stories of successful investors and what lessons they can extract from their stories. Even if they choose never to get into investing in stocks or buying shares in companies, the stories will still act as a guiding light in whatever they do.

Chapter 10: Trust Funds and The Introduction of Roth IRA

"Games are won by players who focus on the playing field – - not by those whose eyes are glued to the scoreboard."

Warren Buffett

I am sure we have all heard of Trust Funds. In fact, I mentioned it in one of the earlier chapters, and we must look deeply into it.

However, I did not cover the Roth IRA and how it, alongside Trust Funds, is a key component of building and maintaining wealth for anyone who desires it.

As with any other financial lesson we have learned in this book, knowing how to break down the complexities of Trust Funds and Roth IRAs in a manner children can digest is not very easy.

However, this chapter will look at clever ways to introduce these concepts to your children and make them understand how they are key to helping them build wealth.

Deciphering Trust Funds

Trust Funds have long been revered and held in high regard as powerful tools for preserving wealth, providing asset protection, and facilitating asset transfer to future generations. But what exactly is a Trust Fund?

Well, before trying to explain what a Trust Fund is to a child, it is important that you also understand it.

A Trust Fund is a legal entity where you put assets or property on behalf of a person or organization. The Trust Fund is under the management of a trustee named at the Trust's inception.

The assets in the Trust Fund will often remain there until certain circumstances are met, at which point the assets will then be distributed to their beneficiary.

So, how do you explain this to a child?

Well, tell your children that a Trust Fund is like a special container where someone, for example, you, the parent, puts money or valuable items to save for future use.

You can create an analogy by saying it would be like having a piggy bank into which you frequently put money that they can use when they grow up, for example, when they need to pay for college or buy a new house.

After understanding what a Trust Fund is, the next question your kids will probably ask is its benefits.

Benefits of a Trust Fund

A Trust Fund will often have numerous benefits, and below are some of the benefits you can highlight to your child:

Security

The biggest benefit of setting up a Trust Fund is that it guarantees that assets are properly taken care of and are free from usage for any other purpose until the conditions agreed upon when setting up the Trust Fund are met.

Let the child know that money in a trust fund has legal protection from any interference. Thus, nobody will ever touch or use it for any purpose other than its original intent.

Let them know that, for example, when you put money for them in a trust fund, and the money is for them to get into college when they turn 18, nobody will touch that money until they turn 18.

Since they are the beneficiary and you are the parent, you are the one who will set the conditions that must be met before the funds are released. In this instance, the condition is them turning 18, so only when they turn 18 will the Trust Fund be opened and the money or assets accessed.

Provides Inheritance

Trust funds also help provide an inheritance for the children or close beneficiaries of the person who sets up the trust fund.

Let the child know that when you set up a Trust Fund and put assets in it, they will receive these assets from you after a designated period. Unlike a will, however, they can access the assets in the Trust Funds during your lifetime as long as the agreed conditions are met.

For example, if the agreed conditions are that the child has access to the Trust Fund when they reach 18, and if they do it when you are still alive, they will still receive the assets.

Tax benefits

Trust Funds are a fundamental part of wealth management and preservation because some types of trust funds also provide varied tax benefits.

An irrevocable trust is an example of a trust that offers tax benefits to the person who set it up. Let the child know that this type of Trust Fund is often set up for family members under age 18, the financially dependent, or those with special needs, and the assets within the trust are protected from creditors.

But why teach your child all this, I hear you asking?

When it comes to building wealth, your child's understanding of what a Trust Fund is, how it operates, and its benefits helps them not only do the same when they reach adulthood and are building their wealth but also helps them know what to expect if you have also left them some assets in their Trust Fund.

Understanding and Breaking Down Roth IRA

A Roth IRA is one of the most important contributions anyone looking to create wealth should consider putting their money into.

Before looking at how you can introduce this concept to your child and its benefits, let us first explain the Roth IRA and how it functions to you so you know how to explain it to the child.

A Roth IRA is one of the best contribution platforms because it has no restrictions on a person's age before they start investing. Any child aged 17 and younger can contribute to a Roth IRA as long as they can prove that they earn an income.

And when we say earn an income, it could be salaries, tips, or any other taxable employee compensation. It could also include net income from being self-employed.

So, if your child has started taking W-2 (Wage and Tax Statement Form) jobs during the long summer holidays, such as working at a grocery store or perhaps as a caddie at a golf course like Peter Lynch, they are legally eligible to contribute to a Roth IRA.

It could also come from other jobs such as babysitting, dog walking, and yard work. Even infants could be eligible to contribute to a Roth IRA if they earn an income, for example, through modeling. If you've seen infants and other babies in commercials, they qualify for Roth IRA contributions.

Now, I hear you asking about allowances or cash gifts. Don't they count as income? Gifts and allowances do not count as income, at least not according to the IRS. However, you and the child can agree to claim that the money you paid them was for work they did for others, such as lawn mowing or chores.

Before deciding to teach about and open a Roth IRA account for your child, you should know the rules attached to opening an IRA for a child. These rules give you a view of withdrawal rules, tax implications, contribution limits and eligibility.

Custodial Roth IRA eligibility

As I mentioned, eligibility for Roth IRA contributions has no age restrictions as long as the child earns what the IRS defines as 'taxable income.' That means income generated from working any job or running a business (Self-employed).

Custodial Roth IRA Contribution Limits

The limit contributions for Roth IRA for children as of 2023 is the total annual earned income or $6,500, whichever is less. So, for example, if the child earns $4000 a year baby sitting, they are allowed to contribute up to $4000 to a Roth IRA.

Anybody can contribute to the Roth IRA if the child has already earned income that qualifies them to contribute. Then, the parent could make the other deposits for them or match their child's contributions to the Roth IRA.

Custodial Roth IRA Tax Implications

When you open a Roth IRA account for your child, it is funded with after-tax dollars, meaning they save already taxed monies. So, when they are ready to withdraw that money during retirement, they won't pay any tax (unless under certain circumstances, as we will see below).

Custodial Roth IRA Withdrawals

The rules for withdrawing from the Roth IRA for children are that:

- If the account has been open for at least five years, the account owner can withdraw the contributed money without taxes or penalties. They don't even need to have a good reason for withdrawing.

- Withdrawing money earlier than five years means the money may be taxable and could be subject to early withdrawal penalties.

- Money withdrawn early for medical disability or purposes such as purchasing a first home will not attract taxes or penalties.

- Money in an IRA can be withdrawn for use for qualified education expenses. The withdrawal will not attract any penalties, but the earnings will attract income tax.

So, how do you explain a Roth IRA to a child?

Well, teach the child that a Roth IRA is a special account they can use to save money for use when they are older. Let them know that it is a way of saving money now for later use when they have stopped working and have no other source of income.

So, unlike other saving types, in this type of saving, they aren't saving it to spend on one particular thing but rather to use the savings as a source of income when they retire from active work and have nothing earning them money.

Here is an example to use (you can also think of other analogies):

A Roth IRA account is like a magical jar where you put some money, and then, when you are older and perhaps don't get any allowance from me anymore, the money you put in this magical jar will be useful and ensure you still have money to spend.

Benefits of Roth IRA

There are several reasons why opening a Roth IRA account for your child is massively beneficial to them, such as:

Gets them Started Early on Retirement Savings

It is unconventional, but getting your child started early on saving for their retirement might give them a massive head start that helps them build wealth and live in bliss post-retirement.

Let the child understand that the money they put in the Roth IRA account is a great investment because it will come in handy when they are older and cannot work anymore.

Grows their Money

Explain to the child that money they put in a Roth IRA will often compound over time, and thus, when they grow older, they have more money to use. Take them back to the analogy of the tree and compounding interest. If they plant a tiny seed and it grows into a tree, they get fruits and, thus, many seeds from it.

And this compound interest will only grow larger with the child starting early. While most people who start their Roth IRA account as adults will save for around 30-40 years, when you start your child early with their contributions, they will have about 50 years or more of tax-free growth of their Roth IRA money due to compound interest.

Thus, let them understand that if they start saving in their Roth IRA account early in life, they are on their way to accumulating a good amount of money when they retire.

Low-Income Tax

Roth IRAs will often be most beneficial when they make contributions at a lower tax rate and anticipate rising to a higher tax rate when they begin making withdrawals.

That means when your child starts contributing to the Roth IRA account, they will attract lower fees than they would if they set up the account as adults. Then, when they decide to wait for retirement to withdraw, they will pay a higher tax rate but will have more left due to their early start.

Practical Lessons on Understanding Taxes and Money Management

Starting a Roth IRA account means you will need to get your child a Social Security number and another tax identification number.

With these things, your child gets to put into practice the lessons you taught them about money management and taxes. For example, they will learn to fill out W-2 and 1099 forms under your guidance, giving them financial competency early in life.

Trust Funds and Roth IRAs seem like things for the very wealthy, but they are fundamental things to know about and begin to invest in when looking to start your child on the fulfilling path toward building wealth.

A Trust Fund will be where your child will acquire their inheritance from you, thus getting them a head start in the journey towards wealth creation.

On the other hand, a Roth IRA account will set them up for life if they choose to continue saving into the account until retirement, thus ensuring they live a life of plenty in old age even with no income source.

You can set up a Trust Fund and a Roth IRA account for your child even if you aren't wealthy, so, on top of teaching your child about them and their benefits, begin to create a Trust Fund and open a Roth IRA account for them.

Rich people give their children a head start in life with Trust Fund and Roth IRA, so if you get a chance, give yours a head start too, even if it is not much.

Chapter 11: The Daddy Excuse–Family Background Shouldn't Stop Wealth Building

"The first step toward success is taken when you refuse to be a captive of the environment in which you first find yourself."

Mark Caine

Reading stories of some of the most successful people throughout history, a major theme you will notice is that some of them grew up in families that weren't well-off. In fact, some of them grew up in extreme poverty.

Andre Carnegie, who many consider America's most influential steel magnate, was born to an ordinary family in Dunfermline, Scotland. The family shared a cottage with another family, with both families sharing the eating area.

They struggled to make ends meet, and when Carnegie was 12, his family decided to move to Allegheny, Pennsylvania, in search of a better life. Here, Carnegie would get his first job: changing spools of threads in a cotton mill.

He would then move from this job to becoming a telegraph manager before moving to railroads when he was 18. Here, he still worked the telegraph but also got to experience the growing rail industry. It was here that his interest in rail and steel grew.

Peter Lynch was also not privileged in his early life. After losing his father early to cancer, he had to start working to help his mother support the family.

Many of us blindly believe that because we haven't had the luck of being born into obscene amounts of wealth, we do not have what it takes to become wealthy and to create our generational family wealth.

I call this thinking type the 'Daddy excuse.' This thinking goes like this:

Because my parents weren't wealthy, I also will not become wealthy. More than anything, this line of thinking is the primary cause of why many people are born, raised, and then, later in life, die without ever attempting to improve their lives and do better than their parents.

You do not have to give your children the same kind of upbringing you had. I am certain that many people who adopt a 'daddy excuse' attitude don't do that because they do not like the idea of building wealth. I believe that many just never learned proper financial literacy early in their lives.

So, now that you know better, you should be the person who ensures that your child does not grow up with such an attitude. You are the person who needs to ensure that your child grows up believing they have what it takes to create, build, and maintain generational wealth.

How to Help Children Break Free From The Daddy Excuse

Below are a few ways you can urge your kids to take full control of their financial future regardless of their upbringing and financial struggles:

Share Your Personal Story

Children relate very well to information we share with them through stories, so to help encourage them to become a lot more willing and happy to build wealth, share your story with them.

Share with them your previous financial struggles, and don't be shy about letting them know that you grew up in abject poverty. Be candid and heartfelt in how you share your story.

The story will let them know that determination, will, and grit are the only ingredients they need to overcome any hurdle. Let them know that everything you own came from your sweat and blood.

But more importantly, the story will let them know that if they grew up lacking but can now afford many things, then they are doing better than you, and going on to build wealth is not that hard.

Share the Importance of Early Financial Education

Sometimes, your children might feel you are teaching them something they do not need to know at that age, but you need to let them know of the profound impact of early financial literacy and knowledge.

Let them understand that starting their finance journey early is as important to building wealth as finding a good job or creating that financial discipline.

One of the best qualities you can teach kids about building wealth is the value of time. As we have seen from some stories of some of the world's most successful entrepreneurs and investors, many started their journey very early in life, with some even getting started when they were barely teenagers.

Sure, some people become overnight millionaires, but these stories are the exception, not the norm; let your child understand this.

Thus, your child should understand that equipping themselves with essential financial skills from a young age will put them on the right path towards building wealth because it will afford them more time to make more savings or quickly recover from mistakes.

Encourage Self-Reflection

After laying down the foundations of a proper financial education, please encourage your children to reflect on the lessons and the decisions they make with their money.

While children might understand that they are not from a wealthy family, they should be able to self-reflect and understand that, with the knowledge you have taught them, they can make the correct financial decisions to change the narrative.

After each expenditure, they should always look back at it and reflect on how they spent that money. Was that the right financial decision? Should they have spent that much on that product? Is the product giving them proper value for money?

Doing this prompts them to think about times when they wished they knew more about money and could make better financial decisions. Please consistently encourage them to go through the wrong financial decisions they had previously made. Would they want to repeat that?

Such self-reflection encourages the child to learn how to take responsibility and not look for excuses when they need to make the right financial decisions to build wealth.

Set Goals Together: Or At Least Be Their Guide

To ensure your child takes in all the financial lessons and does not default to making poor excuses, help them set financial goals.

While it might be tempting to leave the child to their own devices once you are confident they have absorbed all the financial lessons you have taught them, you must remain present to offer them guidance and direction in every possible way.

Remember that they are still children; thus, even if they begin to show some financial initiative by setting financial goals and whatnot, you should always be around to help them through the process.

Sure, the child can decide they want to buy something without your input, but you should ensure they understand that they should run that decision through you before making the purchase.

Your child could, for example, decide that they want to buy themselves a smartphone because they feel they need it. Now, for a child in their teens or getting into high school, this is a reasonable purchase, which is okay. Then, you can guide them on the best smartphone to buy while still saving money, the best place to buy one, and so on.

However, if your child is in middle school or even lower and wants to use their savings to buy a smartphone, that is a bit too early. Thus, by running the decisions through you, you should be able to tell them why that is a bad idea and then help them think of a different, more valuable way to spend the money.

When you are there to guide them, you ensure they do not have any excuse not to make better and wiser financial decisions when you are not around.

Empower Them to Action

Taking action is one of the most significant things anyone, including your child, can do.

While you are teaching them financial literacy to the best of your ability, please also encourage them to take further action that can help them in their journey toward a bright financial future.

For example, if it gets to a point where they feel as though the allowance you are giving them is not enough to cover the financial goals they have in mind, empower them to begin looking for summer jobs or starting a small business.

Research what it takes to run a small lawn mowing business or the requirements for becoming a store clerk and then encourage them to apply for that job or start that business. Help them draft the CV that will earn them a job, and help them build a portfolio for their business, perhaps by having them work for some of your friends, who will then recommend your child's business to others. Help them draft a letter requesting a permit to run a small business.

Taking action is a critical part of building wealth. One might have all the knowledge in the world and the best budget and business understanding, but if they do not put all this knowledge into action, then it is all useless.

Thus, be encouraging and help them put into action what they have learned so they begin the journey towards wealth building early and have no excuse not to make better financial choices when they are adults.

Provide Positive Reinforcement

For your child or children to be a lot more willing to absorb and apply the lessons you teach them, please be there to provide them with positive reinforcement for making the right financial decisions.

Celebrate their successes, no matter how small, and reinforce the importance of financial education, even as you encourage them to continue learning.

For example, if the child has saved a lot throughout the year, you could provide them with positive reinforcement by giving them additional finances as a congratulatory message for their good work in the savings.

Positive reinforcement builds your child's confidence and motivates them to continue down the path they have chosen, thus allowing them to let go of whatever excuses they have been holding onto from the past.

Be a Positive Role Model

Finally, being a positive role model is very important when it comes to getting rid of daddy excuses.

No one ever wants to be born into, grow up in, and then die in poverty. At the very least, every one of us wants to die in a better place than the place where we were born.

Unfortunately, not many of us manage to let go of the excuse that our birthplace is the thing holding us back.

Someone might decide that since they were born into a less privileged family, they have no way out. They put little effort into learning more about finances and no effort into trying to save or start a business and grow it.

They spend their time stating that they cannot do better financially because their family is not wealthy, hoping for some sympathy. Unfortunately, some of us transfer this kind of thinking to our children.

When the child sees you are always complaining, always giving excuses on why you can't do ABC, always unable to save or make the right financial decisions, then they will pick up on that and do that, no matter how many times you attempt to teach them the theory of financial literacy.

Thus, the most important action you can take to break your children out of their 'daddy excuse' is to become a good role model.

I would suggest that, if you are struggling with your past, self-acceptance, and the role your choices have played in your financial situation, try to sort these out first before attempting to teach your child financial literacy.

Let go of your excuses about the past. Forgive your parents for not teaching you about financial literacy early in life. Let go of the wrong financial choices you have been making. Begin to save more, spend more wisely, and put your money into wealth-building portfolios such as bonds and stocks.

Becoming a good role model to your child is probably the best lesson you can give them because children, even the rebellious ones, will always seek their parents' approval and pick up on their behavior, even though subconsciously.

Thus, always strive to embody what you teach the child so they understand you practice what you preach. Your actions mean more to a child than your words and are what your child will take in the most.

Not all of us will be born into rich families, which is okay. It is up to us to learn about making the right financial choices and then pass on these lessons to our children so we can change the narrative and create a lineage of generational family wealth.

Conclusion

Building wealth and creating a future generation of privilege is a journey that some of us, unfortunately, never get to undertake. Some of us are born, grow up in, and die without ever attempting to improve the situation we were born into.

In this book, I have aimed to teach parents how to get their children started early on financial literacy so they can give their children an edge in building wealth and changing the narrative.

Throughout this exploration, we have delved into intricacies of financial concepts such as how a poor child and a rich child will often not differ much in terms of their dreams and aspirations but differ significantly on financial literacy; why the thought that money is evil is what's keeping us poor and how to change this attitude to embrace the love of money.

We have looked into financial lessons around budgeting, how to spend wisely, how you can teach your child the concept of money based on house chores, and how they can dream big and free themselves from their background in their desire to build wealth.

I also hope the financial lessons you can teach your child at home come in handy, and I also hope the understanding of Trust Funds and Roth IRA pushes you to do the best you can for your child.

I anticipate that this book will become the catalyst for you and your child to begin the journey toward building wealth for the family, and I wish you all the best as you get down to this endeavor.

The journey won't be easy, but it will be worth it. All the best!

Other Books By The Author

Rich Nurse Poor Nurses: https://mybook.to/Richnursepoornurses

Don't be child BFF: Be a parent: https://mybook.to/Beaparent

The Real Issues in Nursing Stress and Mental Illness: https://rb.gy/f17m19

The Real Guide to Teenage Depression: Handling Teen Depression: https://mybook.to/Esyqy

Becoming travel nurse: https://mybook.to/travelnurse

Positive self-parenting: https://a.co/d/88abQqr

How to make it in nursing as a man: https://mybook.to/malenurses

Mindfulness Journey: Loving Your Inner Child Replace a Negative Mindset with Healing That Comes from Love: https://mybook.to/replacenegative

Molding my destiny: https://mybook.to/mydestiny

Warm Hearts: https://mybook.to/warmhearts

The Journey To Respect starts with You: https://mybook.to/journeytorespect

The Great Big Slap: https://mybook.to/thegreatbigslap

Everything I never told you: https://mybook.to/motherconfession

Wish You Knew The Family Wanted Your Love: https://mybook.to/wishyouknew

© Patrice M Foster

Learn More About Patrice M. Foster From:

https://patricemfoster.com

www.ingramcontent.com/pod-product-compliance
Lightning Source LLC
LaVergne TN
LVHW091303080426
835510LV00007B/366

www.ingramcontent.com/pod-product-compliance
Lightning Source LLC
LaVergne TN
LVHW091303080426
835510LV00007B/366